Miracle Platform Power:
The Psychology of Successful Speechmaking

Also by the Author:

Sell Like an Ace—Live Like a King!
The Wrong Target
Drilling for Death

Miracle Platform Power:
The Psychology of Successful Speechmaking

Howard

John Wolfe

Parker Publishing Company, Inc.
West Nyack, N.Y.

Library of Congress Cataloging in Publication Data
Wolfe, John Howard.
   Miracle platform power.

   Includes index.
   1. Public speaking. I. Title.
PN4121.W53   808.5'1   79-9220
ISBN 0-13-585513-6

Printed in the United States of America

Dedication

To the speakers of America
and, even more,
to the audiences.

Too often, they've deserved better—
Here's hoping this book helps them get it.

What Miracle Platform Power Will Do for You

This is not a book on how to speak; it's a book on *how to get people to listen*. After more than 20 years on the professional speaking circuit—and over 2,500 addresses throughout most of the Free World—I'm convinced that this is the viewpoint we *must* take if we want our talks to go over bigger with audiences. For the *audience* is the only thing that counts. It's not what you say—not even how you say it—but how the audience *receives* it. That's what *Miracle Platform Power* is all about.

I first realized this at college, when I helped earn my way through Dartmouth as a part-time magician at resort hotels throughout New England. Magic was really big-time in those days, and like all the other devotees of that era, I spent hours every day in front of a mirror, practicing all the finger-flinging maneuvers I'd learned at the feet of the masters.

But then, after a few years, I suddenly began to notice my *audiences*. And I saw that to *them* the magic itself was totally unimportant! Nobody seemed to care what I had up my sleeve; they only cared whether *they* enjoyed the end result! If there was

7

any "trick" at all, it was just getting the *audience* to like what they saw. *That* was the miracle!

Exactly the same thing is true in public speaking: *What you say and how you say it are totally unimportant—except in terms of how your message is received by the audience.*

And that's how *Miracle Platform Power* will make a world of difference in the way you're accepted by your listeners. What you'll find here, if you put it to use, will determine whether your next talk gets you a polite smattering of applause or a standing ovation—again, because throughout these pages we'll be looking at public speaking strictly through the eyes and ears and emotions of the *audience.*

This is why we'll be debunking some age-old theories you may have read in the past. We'll be talking only about what really matters to the *audience*—because that's the only thing that should matter to *you* as the speaker.

And this brings up another important point revealed in this book: Just as the audience is more important than the speech, so is the *speaker!* It's how you handle *yourself* on the platform that determines the response you're going to get. Not your message. *You.*

This is why *Miracle Platform Power* concerns itself with the *psychology* of successful speechmaking. Not that there's any pseudo-scientific mumbo-jumbo in the book. There isn't. But you *will* find the subtle "tricks of the trade" that make the difference in how well you go over—methods you can use to command an audience like a pro. .

Here, for example, are just a few of the audience-tested tips you'll get in this book—tangible techniques that will bring you more applause every time you get up to speak:

Chapter 2 unveils a unique two-step method to rehearse your speech—so you *know* it'll come out the way the audience likes it.

Chapter 5 presents seven sure-fire ways to get the audience on your side the minute you stand up to talk.

And then Chapter 10 offers a miraculous way to get more applause when you finish. (Even most of the real pros don't know this one!)

How to get bigger laughs is covered in Chapter 6—including exactly what to do *after* the laugh for best audience response.

Did you ever have something go wrong during a speech? (I have!) Chapter 8 tells you how to handle these bugaboos without losing your listeners.

And Chapter 9 provides a simple, never-fail way to make the audience like *you* better than your speech!

So it doesn't really matter what kinds of audiences you address, to whom you speak or how often. If you want to *improve* your public speaking effectiveness—and I assume you do or you wouldn't have read this far—then *Miracle Platform Power* is for you. Not because I say so. Because your *audiences* will. And they make the difference.

John Wolfe

Contents

Ready-Reference Story-Teller's Guide, *cont'd.*

Miracle Platform Power:
The Psychology of Successful Speechmaking

1

The Professional
Approach
To Platform Power

What Makes a Pro a Pro?

Let's start out with one basic premise: Every speaker who has ever faced an audience *can* improve his Platform Power. No matter how good (or bad) you are now, you can be better. The same principle obviously applies to every other endeavor; that's why winning football teams still have coaches.

My second premise may be a bit harder to swallow: You can probably improve your speaking ability *more* than almost any other activity, simply because most speakers—even many experienced veterans—are normally so terribly bad!

17

Let me give you just one example for openers.

Almost 20 years ago, I was privileged to attend a special testimonial dinner sponsored by the prestigious Sales Executives Club of New York. It was a gala black-tie affair, held in the grand ballroom of the Waldorf-Astoria.

The guest of honor and feature speaker of the evening was the chairman of the board of one of America's top blue-chip corporations. As an ex-Air Force ace, he was a man I almost worshipped. (I happen to be a flying nut.) And, being in the public eye, he was often called upon to address large audiences.

As the saying goes, there were only three things wrong with his speech: 1) he read it; 2) he read it badly; and 3) it wasn't worth reading.

Honest, it was *pitiful* to see one of the most famous and respected individuals in the world, a fearless and dynamic leader of men, falling flat on his face!

The problem was not that he was an amateur, but that he was *amateurish*. And that's what this first chapter is all about.

Webster defines a professional as "one who makes his living by his art, as distinguished from an amateur." One does something for money; the other does it for free. Hence, there are pro vs amateur golfers, football players, sleight-of-hand tricksters—and speakers.

But Miracle Platform Power involves another vital factor—the professional *attitude*. This has nothing to do with money. It's the approach, the style, the flair—and, yes, the degree of *perfection*—that the pro brings to his work. So, whatever you do for a living, whoever pays your salary, this is the first element you need for Miracle Platform Power.

Of course, attitude involves other things—how you prepare your speech, how you rehearse, how you open, how you close, how you use humor, showmanship, props and visual aids and so forth. All of these directly affect the psychology of audience reaction, which is why they're all covered in this book. However, the main ingredient of a professional attitude is simply a matter of recognizing the *importance* of professionalism in the way you conduct yourself in front of that audience.

How you conduct yourself the rest of the time is *not* important. Some columnists have complained that Johnny Carson is rarely the suave, witty charmer in private that he is on the air. I say, "So what!" He doesn't have to be; that's not what he's paid for. His only job is to give a sparkling performance while he's on camera. Anything he does before or after the show matters to the rest of us only to the degree that it adds to, or detracts from, that 90-minute segment of air time.

Similarly, when you get up to address a group, the only thing that really counts to *them* is what you say and do during your talk.

After all, the intent of this book is not to help you get along better with your wife. It's to help you get along better with *audiences*.

And the first step to Miracle Platform Power is an attitude of *professionalism*.

Professionalism and Audience Psychology

As I said in the Introduction, this is not a "psychological" book in the usual sense—but it *is* about psychology. For while I'm not a psychologist, I do know the psychology of an *audience*.

And this audience psychology we're talking about is not a matter of mystical voodoo. You don't have to be a witch doctor to pull it off. It's simply a matter of *understanding* what audience psychology is all about—and then perfecting the *techniques* to make it work for you.

Take, for example, any top entertainer. What is that "magic" they all seem to project? Part of it, obviously, is sheer God-given talent. You and I have it or don't have it to a greater or lesser degree, and that, admittedly, is something we can't do much about.

But most of any great star's *real* success comes from "playing" to the audience. Which is really another way of saying that he knows his business—and works at it. He commands an audience through *professionalism*.

Several years ago, I attended a giant rally for the United Fund campaign in Houston. The Hughes Tool Company, one of my clients, had arranged for Sammy Davis and his show to appear as the featured attraction, so everybody who was anybody attended. The auditorium was packed with thousands of Houston's leading citizenry.

Now, Sammy Davis had never worked in that theater before. He was there for just that one performance. *But*—and here's my point—everything went off like clockwork. The mikes worked, the band provided perfect accompaniment, and the lights dimmed precisely on cue. Not to belittle Sammy Davis' talent for a moment—it's immense—I still say that this stunning *professionalism* in every phase of the show was largely what brought on the prolonged standing ovation.

Then came the commercial—which was what the whole evening was really all about. This was when the general chairman of the United Fund came on to make his appeal for funds. Here, again, was an extremely prominent man, a strong community leader and—supposedly—a capable speaker. And yet half his speech wasn't even heard because—would you believe this?—the mike wasn't on! His mouth movements made him look like Charlie McCarthy without Edgar Bergen!

This man's job was to enthuse the business community of Houston to support the United Fund. And Houston being Houston, it was a highly successful campaign. But the "psychology" of the chairman's speech was loused up—simply because he didn't *know* enough to check out his mike before using it.

And that's how the "psychology" of successful speech-making depends on professionalism.

Platform Power Works Anywhere

Obviously, better speaking is *important* to you or you wouldn't be reading this book.

You may actually be active on the professional circuit—in which case you'd *better* develop some solid Platform Power or you won't eat regularly!

Or, more likely, you're a business or professional man or woman who's called upon to address audiences on various occasions. Those audiences may range in size from a handful to a large roomful.

It makes no difference. Platform Power—and the psychology of audience response—works anywhere, with any group, of any size. And, conversely, *not* using it *doesn't* work!

When the John Wolfe Institute's headquarters moved to Houston in 1964, our first local client was Houston Natural Gas Corporation, which enrolled 27 men in our 13-week sales course. Since then, they've enrolled dozens more.

One of the important features of our program is the *active participation* it develops among everyone in the group. But one of the men adamantly refused to go along with this vital aspect of the course. The rest of the group cajoled him and I applied all the pressure I reasonably could—I even took him to lunch for a private skull session. All to no avail. The man just couldn't stand on his feet.

Before the course was completed, the company instituted a policy that called upon these salesmen to address meetings of home builders in the area. The man I'm talking about couldn't do it—and was promptly terminated.

Another example:

Recently, I was asked to address the annual sales meeting of the Browning-Ferris Company. They intended to show my film "Sell Like an Ace, Live Like a King" and then have me "step out of the screen" for a live inspirational talk to their 150-man sales force.

As usual, I arrived early to check out the facilities, because this, too, importantly affects the psychology of Platform Power. (Lots more about this in Chapter 4.) The podium was at stage left, the screen was in the center, and the blackboard was at stage right—all as I had asked. And, I made sure, the mike could easily be lifted off the podium and carried to the other side while using the blackboard. Great.

However, the fellow who preceded me on the program—a vice-president of the company—didn't know about such things. So when *he* used the blackboard, the mike was left in its clamp on the podium, and the audience couldn't hear what he was saying! Despite the fact that his message was vitally important!

Here's another example:

I belong to a Rotary Club in Houston (even though my travel schedule prohibits regular attendance). Each week, one of the members gets up to introduce the guests of the day. Almost always, the performance is the same: names are mispronounced, the applause is off-cue, eyeglasses are put on and taken off a half-dozen times and so forth. Please understand that Rotary is a superb organization and its members constitute some of the finest people in the world. I'm not knocking them. But they do louse up the simple business of making introductions!

When I'm asked to handle that chore, it's clearly not a "professional" appearance by Webster's definition, since I'm obviously not paid for that 5-minute stint in front of my buddies. But I still spend an hour or so in preparation. When the guests arrive, I check on the proper pronunciation of their names. As the meal is being served, I transfer the names to a single sheet of paper, printing them phonetically in big block letters so I can read them smoothly without going through the eyeglass routine. If a guy tells me his name is Joe Shape, but it's spelled S-C-H-O-E-P-P-E, I still put down JOE SHAPE, so I can *say* it right. And, when the moment arrives, I give out each guest's hometown and business *before* announcing his name, so the applause will come at the right time.

Now, all of this may sound a bit petty—and perhaps more than a bit cocky. So let me say right now that we all goof *some* of the time, and I've pulled some real beauts over the years. But professionalism is still what we should all strive for—all of the time.

These "little" things add up to the total effect that's created. No matter what kind of speaking you do, or how often, they all apply. Anywhere, anytime.

This is the stuff that Miracle Platform Power is made of.

Professionalism Is Speech Insurance

As I just said, no speaker can achieve absolute perfection *all* of the time. But he or she can sure try—and this is yet another element of platform professionalism. As my public speaking professor at Dartmouth used to say, the difference between an adequate speaker and a great one is his "batting average"—not how *good* he is, but how *often* he's good! This is what makes the real pro.

Again, this principle applies in any endeavor. In baseball, a batter is not judged by how far he hits the ball—nor by how many times he strikes out—but by his *average*. In golf, Jack Nicklaus has been known to card an 82,—but he's paid on the total tournaments he *wins*.

Over the years, I've been a "speakee" as well as a speaker, meaning that I've had occasion to book other speakers in many instances. What I look for is *assurance* of quality—and so does everyone else.

Some years ago, as president of the Sales and Marketing Executives of Houston, I was looking for an inspirational speaker to headline our giant sales rally. (As a member of the club, I obviously couldn't book myself!)

I chose Bill Gove, not because he's one of the very best in the business—which he unquestionably is—but because he's top-notch *every* time he faces an audience. And, again, that's because he does all the things we're talking about.

In my own case, I'm reminded of a talk I gave at a Phillips Petroleum meeting in Fort Lauderdale. It so happened that I had a miserable cold at the time. I sniffled all through dinner the previous evening, slept at most an hour that night, and felt terrible in the morning. But I'd been hired to kick off the meeting with a rousing pep talk. And, at the fee they were paying, that's what they had every right to expect—cold or no cold. So that's what I gave them.

As one of the Phillips brass told me later: "The second you got up to talk, your cold seemed to disappear."

Once more, this is the kind of professionalism we're talking about—a vital ingredient to your own Platform Power.

How to Build Platform Power by Keeping It Hidden

One thing you may have noticed about this professional approach I've been talking about is that most of it takes place "*behind the scenes*." Practically all of the examples I've cited have this in common: they concern the *hidden* factors.

And this, itself, is another important example of the psychological aspect of Platform Power, too.

You see, even if your speech carries a wholly serious message, an audience wants to *enjoy* it. To let them enjoy it, you have to make it *easy* for them to look and listen. And now comes the really crucial point: To make it easy for *them*, you have to make it *look* as if it's easy for *you*! A lot easier than it really is!

This is why, when a speaker fidgets, the audience fidgets. When the speaker appears relaxed, the audience relaxes. When the speaker seems to *enjoy* what he's doing, so does the audience. Again, this becomes possible for you *only* when you've done your homework — when you put into practice all the tips you'll get in this book.

Remember Fred Astaire's seemingly effortless dance routines? They were beautiful to watch, largely because he made them appear so simple. Were they *really* that easy to perform— even for Fred Astaire? Not on your life! Ginger Rogers has stated publicly that one of those movie dance routines went through 58 takes before they got it right! But you and I never saw the first 57— only the last one that was perfect!

As speakers, we rarely have the luxury of "58 takes." We get only one shot at each audience, and we have to do our best *that* time. But we still can do this only when our *effort* remains hidden.

I once conducted a half-day sales seminar for Blue Mountain Industries, held at the beautiful Innisbrook resort near Tampa, Florida. It's a great place for golf and relaxation—except when you're there to *work*.

As usual, I had planned for a mid-morning coffee break—not only for my audience (which is crucial) but for *me*! Because, while everyone else is relaxing, I'm always busy making last-second arrangements for the next session. (Remember, this all has to be *hidden*.)

Which is why, in all candor, I really don't enjoy spending those few moments listening to somebody's favorite Pat-and-Mike joke. Yet, I always seem to be collared by some well-meaning individual with this in mind. No reflection on him; he just doesn't *recognize* the work that's involved.

On that particular occasion, one of my friends was conducting a seminar for another company in an adjoining room, and later—when we were both able to relax—I commented on this "occupational hazard" of our business. He pointed out that it's a compliment when people *don't* realize how hard you're working on a platform. As he put it: "That's what I want engraved on my tombstone: HE MADE IT LOOK EASY."

It seems to me that his remark carries real meaning.

All of this is why my examples in this first chapter have concerned so many things *not* to do. Honest, it isn't because I'm trying to take pot shots at people; we're all human and that's why pencils have erasers. I'm merely pointing out the fact that the zillions of "right" things you and I do on a platform aren't seen—except by another pro!

True professionalism in public speaking is like air conditioning on a hot summer day. It's never noticed. It's not supposed to be. People become aware of it only when it's absent.

The pro makes sure—in everything he does—that the means remain hidden, so the overall effect shines through. As the Latins put it: *Ars est celare artem.* Art consists in hiding art.

MIRACLE PLATFORM POWER CAPSULE

1) Professionalism in public speaking is a matter of attitude:
   <u>Act</u> like a pro and you'll be received like a pro.
2) A professional attitude builds listener acceptance:
   You have to play to the <u>audience.</u>
3) The appeal of Platform Power is universal:
   The details are small—but the <u>effect</u> is enormous.
4) Platform Power professionalism is cheap insurance:
   But it <u>always</u> pays off.
5) Professionalism needs to be worked at:
   The secret is to keep it <u>hidden.</u>

2

Developing Miracle Platform Power Rehearsal Techniques

The Miracle 80/20 Formula

As I suggested in the previous chapter, your command of an audience often depends on a great many seemingly "little" things—most of them are things that your listeners are totally unaware of. And of all these, the most important, without doubt, is your preparation and rehearsal. That's what this chapter is all about.

It's only when you really know what you're going to say and do in front of that audience—and *know* that you know—that you can project the air of confidence which is so necessary if you're going to achieve the reaction you want.

27

This is why those of us who speak for a living never seem to have "stage fright." Not because we're unconcerned, or even totally relaxed. Quite the contrary. (Actually, it's when we begin to think it's *too* easy that we're in greatest danger of goofing.) No, it's simply because we're *ready*.

As another example, I'm reminded again of my days as a professional magician. During one season, my first year out of Dartmouth, I was on a tour of schools throughout California. I had a stage name at the time—Tate Topper—and I'd teamed up with a buddy of mine named Bill O'Leary. So the act was "Topper and O'Leary: Double Deception!" Actually, it was sort of an Abbott and Costello routine done with magic, wherein each of us pretended to louse up the other guy's tricks, and the kids got a big kick out of it.

This required considerable coordination to make sure everything worked out the way it was supposed to. So, we rehearsed the act for weeks on end *before* our first performance. Even then, it was only after a few *more* weeks on the road that we really had it down pat. But we could never have gotten through that first show without the weeks of rehearsal that preceded it.

So the 80/20 Formula means simply this: *80 percent of the time devoted to any speech should be spent in preparation and rehearsal,* long before you get up to talk. The other 20 percent is the time you're *actually in front of the audience.*

If you're going to speak for 15 minutes, this means an hour in the wings; for a 30-minute talk, plan on two hours getting ready; for a 45-minute presentation, you're going to need an entire half-day. Those, remember, are *minimums*. This assumes that you're already familiar with your subject and don't need to do any special research. Try to skimp on this vital aspect of your talk and you're dead; nothing else, in this book or elsewhere, can possibly save you!

Again, the simple fact is that 80 percent of the total sales volume of most companies is brought in by 20 percent of the salesmen, and 80 percent of *their* business usually comes from 20 percent of the accounts they call on. It's the same way in public speaking. You can't get away from it: *The only way to make a speech look impromptu is be sure it isn't!*

It's like a pilot's first solo flight. I don't know if you've ever had that experience; if you have, you know what I'm talking about. Even 40-year airline veterans will tell you there's no thrill to compare with it. In my own case, I've flown single-engine airplanes (and, later, twins) to Canada, the Caribbean, and South America—and most places in between—but I'll never forget the first time my instructor got out and said, "Okay, now *you* take it up, ALONE!"

Scared? Sure! But we all got through our first solo because of the *practice* that preceded it. Take off and land, take off and land, take off and land—ad infinitum.

Now, admittedly, making a bad landing *can* be a bit more critical to life and limb than making a bad speech! But not more critical to your ego!

So—please—follow the 80/20 Formula. It's the only way to come out whole.

Why You Don't Need an Outline

Okay, we're agreed that preparation and rehearsal is vitally necessary. Now, how do you go about it?

In school you may have been taught to start with a formalized outline, the kind that lists the points you want to make according to their relative importance: I . . . A . . . 1 . . . a . . . and so on. This looks very neat indeed—on a piece of paper. But you're not designing a piece of paper, you're preparing a *talk*.

We'll be talking about the use of notes in the next chapter, and I don't want to get too far ahead of the story here. But the essential point I've been making right along is still all-important: Miracle Platform Power depends *not* on what *you* say or do, but solely on what the *audience* sees and hears. Hence, your preparation and rehearsal must be directly aimed at creating the right psychology with your *listeners*. And an outline does *not* help toward this end.

Instead, simply jot down *all the ideas you can think of*—in any form whatever—relative to your subject. You can do this on a yellow legal pad or anywhere else. It doesn't make any difference. When you stand up to talk, the audience won't know whether you listed your thoughts on rag-bond stationery or the side of a barn.

Then, simply *number* these ideas in some logical order, bearing in mind the essential objective of what you want to get across to your listeners. In doing this, be sure to keep in mind the "flow" of your overall message. Like any good stage presentation, your speech should follow an orderly sequence, building from a strong beginning to a powerful climax. It must move *forward* at all times.

This, of course, does not mean that every sentence in your talk should end with an exclamation point. Far from it. Even the most suspenseful Alfred Hitchcock movies have their breathers of comic relief—which further strengthen the moments of sheer terror. If you try to emphasize everything, you emphasize nothing. But, still, your message should *build* throughout.

Finally, all you need to do at this point is rewrite these same thoughts in the order in which they're numbered. That's it. For now, *don't do any more writing*.

In our sales seminars around the country, we devote considerable time to public speaking. Thousands of salesmen, including many from among the top American companies listed in *Fortune*, have told me that this one simple tip for preparing a speech has given them far greater command in front of their audiences—exactly the kind of Miracle Platform Power we've been talking about.

It can do the same for you.

The Miracle of Silent Platform Power

Now comes the really important part of the entire process of preparation—your rehearsal. And I do mean deliberate, painstaking *rehearsal*. There's no other way to get ready for a professional performance. So lock yourself in a room, all alone, and *go through the whole talk*—in full—with gestures. This is *very important*.

Now, admittedly, your wife may prefer to talk about the afternoon bridge game. The kids may want you to toss the football. No matter. I'm not suggesting that you ignore your family, but I am saying—emphatically—that if you want to create Miracle

Platform Power *after* you stand up to speak, you *must* rehearse fully in advance, *with no distractions*.

Exactly where and when you do this is totally unimportant. Just so it gets done.

Many of the pros find it easiest to do their rehearsing late at night, when the rest of the house is asleep—and when the phone isn't ringing. For some of us, this is when the whole world seems at peace, the mind is clear, and full concentration can be applied to the job at hand. (Let's not forget, it's not all that difficult, but it *is* a job!)

All of which brings up the Miracle of *Silent* Platform Power. You surely don't want to incur the wrath of your neighbors (much less your own family) by yelling at the top of your lungs at 2;00 o'clock in the morning! And you might even be reluctant—for obvious personal reasons—to be accused of talking to yourself at any other time of the day, either!

The good news is: *You don't have to rehearse out loud.* In full, yes. With inflections, by all means. And even with gestures, most definitely. But *not* necessarily *out loud*.

For, the fact is that with a little practice, you can "hear" your talk better in your own head than you can any other way. All you have to do is mouth the words silently and listen with your mind! This way, you can visualize the audience and sense their every response. You simply do it *mentally*.

Craig Fecel, of Merrill Lynch, Pierce, Fenner & Smith, is just one of many hundreds of people who have used this technique successfully. Like most folks, Craig used to have doubts as to his ability to command an audience. Now, using the "silent" method of rehearsal, he makes forceful presentations to Rotary Clubs and other civic groups over a wide area—and you can bet this has added a whole new dimension to his income and overall success.

Silent Platform Power can work a miracle for *you* as well!

The Sure-Fire In/Out Step to Miracle Platform Power

In a way, this is the next step in your rehearsal procedure. In another sense, it's what makes possible—and so highly effective— the Silent Platform Power we've just been talking about.

So let's go back a bit.

We've agreed that you're going to spend at least four times as long in preparing and rehearsing your speech as you are in delivering it. You're going to have all your ideas jotted down in logical numerical sequence. And you're going to conduct a full dress rehearsal—silently—all alone, with no distractions.

Again, you cannot practice delivering the speech to your wife, as some novices attempt to do. Why? Simply because a speech is not designed to be given to any one individual, but to an *audience*. (That, obviously, is what makes it *public* speaking!)

While you're holding your dress rehearsal, naturally, other ideas will come to you. You may decide to make some changes. You probably will. You'll think of jokes, anecdotes, and other examples as you go along. Maybe there'll be certain visual aids you'll want to add to strengthen your presentation and make the message even more compelling. Fine. Each rehearsal thereby comes that much closer to your live "opening night" on the platform.

Before we go on, I'd like to toss out one final tip about your "dress" rehearsal. You may find it helpful to actually *dress* for it— in the same pin-stripe suit (or even tuxedo) that you're going to wear on the dais! This puts you in a frame of mind where you can *really* make it come alive! First to yourself, and then later to the audience!

This is what the In/Out Step to Miracle Platform Power is all about.

You see, there are really *two* steps involved in delivering a speech effectively. First, you have to "hear" it the way you want it to sound, and then you have to "interpret" it live in front of your audience. And the better the input, the better the output.

It's exactly like the old cliché among computer operators: "Garbage in, garbage out!"—meaning simply that the world's most sophisticated and exotic computer can never perform its miracles unless the right data is programmed into it to start with.

It's the same way with Miracle Platform Power. You need to "program" *yourself* properly before you can achieve the kind of audience reaction you're looking for.

So, when you rehearse, decide on exactly *how* you want

everything to come out. Think about your opening and closing remarks (which we'll be talking about more in later chapters), your most powerful examples, your major points of emphasis, even that favorite joke you like to tell. Precisely how do you want all these to *sound* to your listeners? What about your gestures and visual aids? How do you want them *seen* by the audience? Once you have made all these decisions—and can actually "hear" and "see" yourself as you want the *audience* to hear and see you—half the battle is won.

Then—and only then—can you rehearse *delivering* the speech in exactly that manner. And *that's* when you'll really begin to see your own Miracle Platform Power take hold with your audiences.

Again, take any top-name entertainer. Do their songs, jokes—even their ad-libs—just "happen" to be delivered with such faultless timing? Not on your life! They *rehearse* their performances, using precisely the In/Out Step we've been talking about.

Even my own film, "Sell Like an Ace, Live Like a King," which has been used to train salesmen for hundreds of the top companies in America, fits the pattern. Sure, I had a script. And, naturally, most of it covered material I was already intimately familiar with. Still, I had to "hear" exactly how I was going to sound in each scene, long before the cameras began to roll, in order to make the words come out right.

Or, to put it very simply, there must be input before there can be output.

There's no other way.

How to Insure Your Miracle Platform Power—In Advance

We've been spending a lot of time talking about what you do *before* your speech actually begins. But that's as it should be. Again, you have to spend a lot of time before your speech begins, too! And, as I've said, the better your preparation, the better the final result.

Now, before we move on, there's one final thing you can do to guarantee your Miracle Platform Power before you actually begin to speak.

Very simply, it's to do *more* rehearsing—on the spot—before the curtain goes up.

Chapter 4, for instance, covers how to create a Platform Power environment. You'll find the tips given there highly beneficial in all your public speaking presentations.

But here's the all-important catch: No matter how meticulously you've planned every detail, you cannot depend on things being set up the way you intended.

Again, let me give you just a couple of examples.

Several years ago, I made a tour of eight major metropolitan areas to introduce my "Selling Aces" program around the country. Each presentation was conducted in the leading hotel of that particular city. I contacted all of these hotels well in advance, and told them exactly how I wanted the room set up. Further, I arrived at each hotel a day early, so I could verify all this with their personnel in advance. I even drew them diagrams. Still, not one room was set up the way I specified!

Another example:

Just recently, I completed eight regional sales seminars for Reed Tool Company, one of America's leading oil tool manufacturers. Again, the required room set-up for each meeting was provided well in advance. The word was sent out throughout every region in the U.S. and Canada. Yet, despite the conscientious efforts of the regional managers in each area, in no case was the room set up *right* when I got there.

So here's how to insure your Miracle Platform Power in advance: *get there early.* At least *one hour* early if at all possible.

What do you do during this one hour? Again, you *rehearse.*

Several years ago, I had the pleasure of appearing on the big annual Dallas Sellarama. One of the major events of its kind in the nation—featuring such celebrities as Ronald Reagan—it's invariably a top-notch professional affair. Why? Largely because it's *planned* that way.

In this case, I was told to arrive *two* hours in advance. Every aspect of the total program was *rehearsed,* long before the thousands of spectators arrived. And this is why, year after year, the affair attracts such large and enthusiastic audiences.

Another example:

In my "Selling Aces" seminars around the country, I use large special cards to illustrate my major points: Start with a Spade; Hit 'em in the Heart; Deal in Diamonds; Cushion 'em with a Club; and the Joker—Do It! All of these need to be revealed—on cue—smoothly and without fumbling or hesitation.

So, even after many hundreds of presentations over the years, I *practice* flipping those cards—on the spot—immediately prior to each performance.

One time, in a Houston hotel, there was a certain beam in the ceiling that interfered with my usual procedure. Would I have recognized this *during* my presentation? No way! Only through that last-minute rehearsal—*with the cards*—was I able to detect the problem and move my props around accordingly. Was it worth the trouble? By all means.

The moral is clear: After all your rehearsal at home, you need a *final* rehearsal on the spot, before you go on.

Once again, your Miracle Platform Power depends on audience psychology—and *that* depends on the perfection of your performance when you stand up to speak.

All of which, again, depends crucially on what you do before you're introduced.

2070679

MIRACLE PLATFORM POWER CAPSULE

1) Preparation is vital:
   The only speech that looks impromptu is the one that isn't.

2) First, jot down all your ideas in any sequence:
   Outlines are for writing, not for speaking.

3) You have to rehearse—but not necessarily out loud:
   Silent Platform Power works miracles.

4) Practice the In/Out Step:
   You have to hear it before you can say it.

5) Never forget that last-second off-stage rehearsal, too:
   It primes you for a better performance.

3

Utilizing the
Platform Power
Psychology of Notes

Learning When to Use Notes

During a recent convention of the National Speakers Association—the leading "trade association" in our profession—I was assigned the topic of speech preparation, and the matter of using notes constituted a major aspect of my presentation. And for good reason. Because your notes—by themselves—*can* help you considerably. Or, even more likely, they can louse you up completely.

Incidentally having made reference to the National Speakers Association, I should point out that, other than being a Charter Member—and, as of this writing, one of the 39 people in the country awarded their special C.P.A.E. designation—I have no direct connection with the organization. But for anyone involved in public speaking, it's a marvelous group to be part of. For further information, you can contact Bill Johnson, Executive Director, at P.O. Box 6296, Phoenix, Arizona 85005.

Anyway, as I was saying, I was asked to conduct the session which dealt with the business of using notes.

I began the discussion by referring to a giant sales rally we'd all attended earlier that week, where five of the greatest speakers in America had addressed some 14,000 people from miles around— and where only *one* of these top pros had used any notes at all!

In that one case, the speaker had a lot of very topical material, with numerous statistics as to our nation's economy and the like. So the notes were appropriate—besides which they fit that particular speaker's style.

But, the rest of these top headliners spoke—for about an hour each—with absolutely no notes at all! And *they* were the men who really brought those 14,000 people to their feet. *They* were the guys with Miracle Platform Power!

So the moral is: *The best way to use notes is not to!* Or, at least, to use as few as possible. For the simple fact is that in most speech-making, notes generally do more to *bar* communication than they do to help it.

When a teen-ager does his homework to the accompaniment of rock-and-roll records, he may tell you that all that blaring noise doesn't get in the way. You know better. It does. To whatever degree he's paying attention to the music (?) he's not paying attention to his studies.

Same way in public speaking. To whatever degree your eyes and your mind and your concentration are on your notes, you're not *communicating* with your audience.

And that, again, is what Miracle Platform Power is all about.

When to Read Your Speech—And When Not To

If there's anything worse than poring over notes during your speech, it's *reading* it to your audience—despite the fact that this is precisely what so many "amateur" speakers invariably do.

Once more, it gets right back to that crucial audience psychology we've been talking about all along.

Miracle Platform Power depends on effective *communication* between you and your audience, and this communication must be a *two-way street*—even when you're the only person actually speaking. Or, to put it another way, you have to talk *with* your audience—not just at them—and you simply cannot do this while you're reading a prepared manuscript.

As always, there are exceptions—which is, of course, the reason for the title I've given to this section:

1) If you're addressing the United Nations, or a joint session of Congress. In cases like these, every single word may have historical impact, and you can't chance any slip-ups.

2) If you've had years of professional broadcasting experience. In this event, you probably can get away with reading any speech, anywhere. (I was on one convention program in Honolulu with William F. Buckley, Jr. He *did* read his speech, but did it superbly. He knows how.)

In all other cases, *don't*.

Think for just a minute about all the times *you* have listened to some character reading a speech. Did you enjoy it? In a very few cases, maybe. In the huge majority, I'll bet you didn't.

It's like hearing a "canned" sales pitch over the telephone—only worse. There simply isn't any *communication* and, hence, the audience psychology is all wrong.

So, whatever you do, don't read from a prepared script. If you want to write to your audience, send 'em a form letter. If you want to talk, *talk*.

There's just one more exception to this general rule:

If, during any presentation, you're quoting briefly from a published source—a newspaper item, magazine article, or whatever—then it's perfectly acceptable, and highly effective, to let the audience know that that's precisely what you're doing. This, remember, does not mean reading your speech as a whole. It means reading just one or two tiny *parts* of it.

In my own sales seminars around the country, for instance, I use a quiz titled "How Persuasive Are You?" that I once wrote for *Reader's Digest*. At that point in the program, I hold up the reprint for all to see, I put on my glasses, and I make it *known* that the item is being read verbatim. This gets the message across better than anything else—and it also lets 'em know for sure that I'm *not* reading the rest of the time.

At the National Speakers Association convention that I referred to a little earlier, one of my friends on the pro circuit told me that he considers it a very special compliment when someone says to him, "You made me feel that you were speaking directly to *me*."

I agree. That's Miracle Platform Power at its best.

You'll never hear that kind of praise when you *read* your speech!

The 3-by-5 Complex—And How to Avoid It

Now to blow another myth about public speaking.

One of the favorite techniques of many amateur speakers (and even a few almost-pros) is to have notes written on 3-by-5 index cards. The theory is that you have each essential thought clearly marked on one individual card. You have the cards meticulously arranged in the order required for your talk, and then, as you finish covering each point, you slide that card to the back of the stack and go on with the next one.

Clever? Sure! Even some books for would-be professionals recommend this procedure. And, as a former magician, I like card tricks as well as anyone!

But is it *effective* in developing the right kind of audience psychology? No!

Why? Because all your fiddling with those cards constitutes still another obstacle to your *communication* with that audience! And if your cards cascade off the podium—which they can easily do—you're dead!

Another problem with index cards is that they lock you in to a canned presentation. After all, Miracle Platform Power depends on how you relate to the *audience*—and, of course, on how they relate to you. If the previous speaker ran overtime, you have to cut your speech short. If the audience seems a little dead, you may have to liven 'em up with a few jokes. Whatever the situation, you have to stay in *command*. And a stack of cards prevents you from doing this.

Going back to the session I conducted at the National Speakers Association convention, several people in the audience commented that this one tip was worth their whole trip! Since then, they've told me it's made a world of difference.

Again, notes should be there to help you develop more Platform Power—not to get in your way.

Miracle Platform Power from One Sheet of Paper

O.K. Now that I've spent most of this chapter emphasizing how *not* to use notes, it's time to talk about how you *can* use notes effectively.

Again, the answer is very simple: Put them all on *one* large sheet of paper (or at most two sheets which you can lay on the podium side by side).

Let's go back a bit. We've agreed that you're going to spend enough *time* in preparation. And we've also agreed that this preparation is going to include a thorough *rehearsal* of your entire speech, so you *know* what you're going to say when you stand up to talk. If you don't, you shouldn't be making the talk in the first place!

That being the case, if you do need notes at all, you certainly don't need many! Maybe just a few "crutches," which highlight the half-dozen (at most) major points you're going to cover. Possibly even a very few sub-points under each one. *But no more!*

Therefore, simply jot down these few notes—in large, easy-to-read block letters—on one sheet (or, as I said, at most two sheets) of standard lined notepaper.

In this way, you have the substance of the entire talk laid out in front of you. No fiddling. No bars to communication. *No hindrances.* It's all right there at a glance!

Again, in our workshops across the country, we've helped many thousands of men and women to achieve Miracle Platform Power. This is one of the priceless tips we've used to do it.

One final point on all this. Once you start using the Single-Sheet Technique, you'll undoubtedly find something else occurring: You'll get to the point where you won't even *look* at these notes at all!

And you'll find that *that's* when your Miracle Platform Power really begins!

Where to Keep Your Notes for Greater Platform Power

Now, for another tip from the pros—one that will make a big difference in your own Platform Power.

It has to do with what we've been talking about all along—the *professional approach* that creates the kind of audience psychology you want.

Again, it's one of those "hidden" factors I referred to in the very first chapter. And, in this case, I mean it literally—keep any notes you have actually *hidden* from view.

You should do this because the audience *wants* you to be in total command. *They* don't want to fidget, so they don't want to see *you* fidgeting!

Therefore, as I say, keep your notes *hidden.*

The ideal way to do this is to place your sheet(s) of notes on the podium *before* the meeting begins. (Still another reason to get there early!) Or, since a previous speaker may cover your notes with his own—which can really louse you up—you can place the sheet(s) flat on the table *next* to the podium, so when you stand up to speak you don't look like a newsboy delivering the morning paper!

But, usually, the easiest, best and *safest* procedure is to have your notes hidden on the shelf *below* the podium surface. (Until everybody else reads this book, you'll always find that valuable space empty—reserved just for you!)

Again, of course, there are exceptions. When the President of the United States walks to the podium at a joint session of Congress, he may be carrying a notebook with him. O.K. Everybody *knows* he's going to read his speech—which, as I said before, is entirely appropriate in that situation.

But it's *not* appropriate for most of us. We need to keep our notes *hidden*, if we have them at all.

Cal Perley, former West Coast radio executive, used to be the executive director of the John Wolfe Institute in Houston. Highly capable, Cal still had trouble remembering four key words used in one of the sessions. I told him the same thing I've been saying here: Use notes if you have to, but don't let anyone *see* you use them.

So, Cal worked out the perfect solution. Before that particular session began, he'd write those four words *in chalk* on the horizontal tray below the blackboard! Nobody was ever the wiser!

Just to explain further, if all this sounds a bit contrived—or even deceptive—let me say right now that it's both! But strictly for the *effect* on the *audience!* Which, once more, is what Miracle Platform Power is all about.

To sum up, your performance in front of an audience is only as flawless—or as loused up—as you make it appear to *them*. And, whatever you can do to *appeal* to that audience (within the limits of good taste, of course), is what you *must* do.

Referring once more to the National Speakers Association convention in Phoenix, one of the attendants at my Workshop said that he'd been taught to let the audience *know* when he goofed, so they'd have more "sympathy" for him.

That's his opinion. It isn't mine.

P.S. I received the coveted C.P.A.E. award.

P.P.S. He didn't.

MIRACLE PLATFORM POWER CAPSULE

1) Eliminate notes wherever possible:
   The fewer your notes, the better your communication.

2) Don't read your speech:
   Talk with your audiences—not at them.

3) Avoid the 3-by-5 complex:
   You're there to speak—not to do card tricks.

4) Put all your notes on a single sheet of paper:
   Then you can begin to throw them away!

5) Whatever you do, don't let notes be seen:
   If you have to have them, have them hidden.

4

How to Create A Platform Power Environment

The Responsibility Is Yours

This is the last chapter in the book dealing with preparation. From here on, we'll be talking about all the things you can do to build favorable audience psychology *after* you get up to speak. Yet, this particular phase of your advance planning—preparing the *environment* for Platform Power—is perhaps the most important of all. And it's also the one most often neglected by speakers.

For the fact is that all of the myriad environmental details surrounding your performance itself can have a highly favorable (or totally devastating) effect on the outcome of your speech. The room, seating arrangements, platform, lectern, microphone, lighting and room temperature are all *crucial* to your success.

45

And the first thing to bear in mind is that *the responsibility is yours*. If something isn't just right, *you* get the blame. So *you* must assume the responsibility for *controlling* the environment to obtain best results.

Let me give you just one example. Some years ago, our Institute created a national sales training program for Arbor Homes, a leading manufacturer of pre-manufactured houses headquartered in Waterbury, Connecticut. As part of the arrangement, I was to introduce the program to all of the dealers from around the country, at a major meeting in New Haven.

As always, I arrived the previous evening to check out the facilities. As soon as I signed in, I introduced myself to the manager of the motel and asked to see the meeting room. He proudly showed me the grand ballroom, which was set up with long tables arranged *perpendicularly* to the platform, with all chairs at a 90° angle to the front. This way, everyone would be looking over his shoulder to see what was going on. I told him I wanted the tables turned around so that the audience would be *facing* me, which he said was no problem.

Then came the tough part.

I asked the manager where lunch would be served, and he said right there in the same room. Same room! That's terrible! During a day-long meeting, people have to get *out* of the room for lunch—besides which, I don't like clattering dishes interrupting my presentation!

The manager agreed that they could serve lunch in another room, but that it would cost an extra $75 for the use of the additional space. Further, he said, the sales promotion manager of the company, who had made all these arrangements, had instructed him *not* to serve lunch in any other room. And my problem, of course, was that *I* hadn't actually been hired to fiddle with these details (as I am in many cases)—and none of the Arbor Homes brass had arrived as yet, so I couldn't confer with *them*.

I knew, nevertheless, that it was *my* responsibility to put on a resultful meeting. So, I told the manager to go ahead and set up the other room for lunch, and that if the client wouldn't go for the extra $75, *I'd pay it myself.*

The punch line to all this is that the sales promotion manager of the company was pretty upset that I had meddled with his carefully laid plans. But the President of Arbor Homes, Paul Posin, was highly grateful. He gladly paid the motel that extra $75—and he also gave *me* considerably more business.

Please understand: I'm not claiming any great genius for *knowing* that the lunch should have been served in a separate room. I am saying, however, that I had the sense to *do* something about it.

As Alan Cimberg, one of the top sales training pros on the circuit, put it to me recently, "When I'm on the platform, whether for an hour or a day, that time is *mine*. Sure, the client is paying for it. But it's up to *me* to put on a top-flight performance."

So, the next time you're asked to speak somewhere, you *don't* have to work under conditions as they may have been planned by the chairman.

The environment is critical. And the *responsibility* for that environment is *yours*.

How to Guarantee a Standing-Room-Only Audience

This gets right back to the audience psychology we've been talking about all along. The fact is that while audiences are made up of *individuals*, they react more favorably to any performance when they're in a *crowd*. This is why a comedian's nightclub routine rarely sounds as funny to you on a record as it does live. So, the more your audience is crowded—within reason, of course—the better their response to your speech, and the bigger your applause.

Therefore, in planning any sort of meeting, choose a room that is *just large enough*. If anything, let it be *too small*. (Again, as the speaker, this is *your* responsibility.)

Along these same lines, try to *avoid high ceilings*. Most hotels, for instance, have imposing ballrooms—which are great for large crowds. For smaller groups, sliding dividers are often used to create smaller spaces. But these dividers don't lower the ceiling! So, pick a room that's the right size to start with—in *height* as well as length and width.

Most important in this same connection, *don't allow too many chairs in the room.* If the program chairman tells you that the expected audience is 100, *you* tell *him* to arrange chairs for 75. If he insists that 500 will be on hand, tell him to plan for 400. Whatever the number, *set up fewer chairs than the size of the expected audience.*

The problem, of course, is that if you have too many chairs in the room, *the empty ones will always be in the front!* Despite the earnest pleadings of the program chairman, people will *not* generally move from the back of a room to the front row—unless they *have* to! Which, again, is why it's *your* job to see that they do—simply by having fewer chairs than people.

Naturally, there's an exception to all this. That's when you have an absolutely captive audience—a company sales meeting, for instance. If there are 50 salesmen working for the outfit—and they all know that the only alternative to showing up is to clean out their desks in the morning—then you can count on most of them being there.

Otherwise, for virtually any other type of affair, it's best to follow the rule I've outlined. If additional seats have to be brought in at the last minute, fine! Again, this is good audience psychology. *Empty* chairs—especially in the front—are very bad. Bad for you *and* the audience.

Remember: It's far better to have people without chairs than it is to have chairs without people!

Capitalizing on "Herd-Instinct" Psychology

An important corollary to what we've been talking about is: *Don't have people spread too far apart.* If the folks in your audience are at a distance from one another, they'll probably remain—and react—as individuals. Crowd them *together*, and they'll respond accordingly.

Similarly, don't have them too far away from *you*. For almost any type of gathering, you should be no further away from the front row (or front tables) than 4-6 feet. That way, you com-

municate better than you do across a wide gulf of empty floor space.

As I've said before, *you* have control over this!

So, if you arrive at the meeting room and find the front row of chairs too far back, simply ask someone to move the back row (or several rows, as the case may be) to the front. This brings them *all* closer! If there are two tiers of tables spread too far apart, have them moved closer together. Or change the set-up completely so that there are three tiers instead of two. (This, again, is why it's important to get there *early!*)

In this same regard, arrange for a stage (or platform) that is high enough so that everyone can see—*but not higher*. If your audience numbers 25, any raised platform is probably extraneous. If you're addressing an audience of 50-100, a 12-inch platform (standard in most hotels) is fine. For 500, you may want one higher.

Again, the idea is to get your listeners *close* to you—and *close* to each other.

Perhaps the best example of all this is the procedure followed at the spectacular showrooms in Las Vegas. The folks who run those places are pros! (Considering the salaries they pay their entertainers, they'd better be!)

You've probably noticed that the opulent theater-nightclubs along the Las Vegas Strip are *huge*. But they're also *intimate*. The front tables are placed smack-dab against the stage. The other tables are all jammed as closely together as possible. The waiters barely have room to serve straight-up martinis! But it's all *planned* that way—to bring as *many* people together as possible, as *closely* as possible.

In Houston, we have a facility known as the Houston Music Theater. It seats 2800 people—in the round. From the outside it looks like a miniature Astrodome. On the inside, it's spacious enough for those 2800 seats, but *all* seats are relatively close to the revolving stage in the center.

So when I was President of the Houston Sales & Marketing Executives Association, *that's* where we held our Sales Rallies. And all the top pros who appeared there—my good friends Heartsill

Wilson and Herb True, among others—said it provided the best audience environment they'd ever experienced.

Admittedly, you may never have an opportunity to dictate quite that sort of room arrangement. There are few places like it in the world. But it's still your responsibility to create the best audience environment possible.

One of my friends, Don Tilden, is a leading spokesman for better health among teenagers. As such, he's addressed many community groups over a wide area.

Don recently told me that at one time he had trouble getting through to his audiences. But now—simply by getting *closer* to the people—he's *communicating* more effectively. His voice is heard louder and stronger, and it's made all the difference in the world.

Again, this is your cue to greater Platform Power—whenever and wherever you speak.

What to Do with Head Tables

This is frankly something I'm a bug about. Hence, a special section on the subject.

The rule is: Unless you *need* a head table to eat off, *get rid of it!* And even when it's necessary to hold food, you still may *not* want to speak behind it.

In my own case, I've addressed (as of this writing) some 2500 audiences. Perhaps in only 100 or so have I spoken behind a head table!

Sure, when I arrive at a meeting room, there's *always* a head table. No matter what you tell the program chairman, and no matter what *he* tells the hotel, some joker in the banquet department always puts it there!

At a trade association convention, for instance—and I've addressed many hundreds—there may be a room set up with 500 chairs. There's a platform at the front. And centered on the platform, with five chairs behind it, there it sits in all its glory—the head table!

Now, what happens if I leave it there? First, several of the chairs will be empty. Second, the few people occupying the other chairs won't know what to do with themselves while I'm speaking. And third—most important as always—the head table is *between* me and my audience and, hence, *bars communication.*

So I get *rid* of the silly thing!

Okay, here's when a head tables *does* make sense:

1) If you're participating in a *panel discussion.* Note that I did not say a meeting where several speakers follow each other on the program. I mean a true panel where *all* are involved at the same time. Then, yes, they all have to be on stage simultaneously—and a head table is indicated.

2) If it's a luncheon or dinner function and you're only making a brief speech—say 20 minutes—using no props or other visual aids.

In all other cases, do *not* speak behind a head table—*ever!*

In the case of a regular meeting, where no food is being served, simply replace the head table with a full-length floor lectern. Ideally, this should be at stage *left* (not center) so you can walk away from it. That is, if you need a lectern at all. I do, not to hold notes, but to hold various props which I use.

In this way, the program chairman stands at the lectern while he's introducing you. Then, as he should, he gets off and *you* hold the spotlight as *you* should!

If it's a meal function—and there *has* to be a head table whether you like it or not—there are still options open for the speaker.

One is to extend the platform on one side and talk from that area. Or, if it's a fairly small group that is set up in the usual "U" shape, why not set up a floor lectern at the *opposite* end—in the open end of the "U"—and speak from there?

I was on a program for Binswanger Glass Company with Bill Gove. I had one of the morning sessions and Bill did the luncheon.

As usual, I eliminated the head table entirely. Bill couldn't, since he spoke at lunch. So, he set up a mike in *front* of the head table and spoke from there.

The point is the same one I've been trying to make right along. Miracle Platform Power is—and must be—a matter of *communication* between you and your audience.

Anything that might get in the way must be gotten rid of. Like head tables.

Temperature and Lighting Control

Temperature and lighting control are two factors of the Miracle Platform Power environment which are often overlooked. Yet, they can be vital to the reaction of your audience.

If the room gets too warm, people tend to tire more quickly. Both you *and* the audience will start to go to sleep. Therefore, be sure to *set the thermostat down*—around 70°. Live bodies will heat the place up, anyway. And, if the room remains a little on the cool side, that's even better.

Remember, *it's far better to have the room too cool than too hot.*

It's the same way with lighting: *It's far better to have too much light than too little.*

The fact is that most meeting rooms are poorly lighted. They're usually designed more for cocktail parties than for speeches. They generally have soft lights in the ceiling—and none on the stage! So, again, it's *your* job to see that proper lighting is installed for your presentation.

Some years ago, I addressed a sales meeting of the Vent-Master Corporation, a leading manufacturer of commercial kitchen equipment. As is often the case, I was scheduled on the afternoon of the closing day—for the final wind-up to an intensive three-day affair.

When I arrived at the meeting room that morning, I saw—as usual—that there was inadequate lighting on the platform. So, during the luncheon break, I had the banquet manager install a special floodlight, hung from the ceiling, to light up the front of the room where I was to speak.

Upon returning from lunch, the sales manager, Bill Johnson (no relation to the Bill Johnson who heads the National Speakers Association), said to me, "Why haven't we had this lighting throughout our three-day meeting?"

I answered (with my usual modesty), "Because you haven't had *me!*"

Another important point about lighting: Just as the audience has to see *you*, you have to see *them* to do your best job.

Remember Al Jolson of vaudeville days? I'm not *that* old, but I do remember the movie! And I had the pleasure of meeting that great star one time when he was entertaining troops in the Pacific.

Jolson was perhaps the first major star to insist that the house lights be turned on. As he put it: "It's not the same *unless I can see their faces.*"

So always make sure to check the "house lights"—as well as the lighting on the platform—before you go on. If you're conducting a seminar-type program, where audience participation is crucial—turn the lights up *full*. If it's a speech, where you're doing all the talking, turn them up *half-way*.

In either case, you have to see the audience. And the audience certainly has to see you!

The Psychology of Selecting Microphones

In the last section, we talked about lighting. As I said, seeing you is vital.

But *hearing* you properly is even more important. Hence, this section on microphone technique.

The cardinal rule is: *Have as much mike as you need—but no more.*

In all candor, when I first started on the circuit, I used to think that a lavalier mike—the kind that hangs around your neck—was *always* the thing to use. Unfortunately, many people still do. A lavalier mike is great when you need it—but an awful nuisance when you don't.

A few years ago, I addressed some 1500 people at a sales rally for the Sales & Marketing Executives of St. Louis. The great Red Motley opened the program and I closed it—with a couple of other speakers slotted in between.

Red was making a *speech* and so was I—so we both used the mike on the lectern. But, one of the other fellows (who apparently felt as I had many years earlier) went through the rigmarole of hanging a cord around his neck—*even though he never moved an inch from behind the podium*. So, all the lavalier mike did was *get in his way.* (Actually, he hit it with his hands a couple of times, so it made funny noises as well.)

So, again, make sure you have the mike that you need—not the one that you don't.

Getting down to cases, there are basically four common types of microphones:

1) The kind that's affixed to the lectern.
2) The kind that stands on the floor.
3) The kind you can hold in your hand.
4) The lavalier, which hangs around your neck.

(A fifth is the new cordless type, but these are expensive and you're not likely to run into them often.)

Now, if you're addressing a small group of about 20 people, you probably don't need any mike at all. For larger groups, you do. And, a mike *does* improve the tonal quality of your voice.

OK, what kind should you use in any given situation? Again, the kind you *need*:

If you're going to remain behind the lectern, use the one that's there. (1)

If you're going to be standing in one place on the floor, get the kind that stands there. (2)

If you're going to be moving around—as you usually should—use the one that travels with you. (3)

And if you're going to need both hands for props and so forth, *then* make sure you have a lavalier so your hands are free. (4)

In any case, be sure to check out the public address system *before* you speak (and before the audience arrives) so you know that the volume and tonal quality are right. This is *crucial*.

Similarly, make sure that any lectern or floor mike is at the right height—just below your face—so you can be heard without being hidden. (If the previous speaker moves it, move it back to the right place before you begin. Then, *leave it alone.*)

If you're using a hand mike, be sure to hold it in the same relative position—just below your face—and *keep it there.* Some inexperienced speakers tend to wave hand mikes around like a wand, thereby causing their voices to drift away into nothingness! Or, they move their heads from side to side, so the sound is constantly rising and falling like a bad telephone connection.

Here's an easy way to avoid falling into this trap.

When you move your gaze to different sides of the room—as you should—*swivel the whole upper part of your body*. This automatically keeps the mike where it belongs!

Simple? Sure! But once again, the difference is like day and night.

And finally, when it comes to putting on a lavalier mike—if that's what you're using—I have one suggestion that may seem to contradict what I've just said: Do *not* put it on just before you begin! (That is, not unless you can put it on *off-stage*, before you appear.)

Again, there's a strong psychological reason for this. The fact is that no matter how much dexterity you possess, hooking up a lavalier mike takes *time*—time when you should be *communicating* with your audience. Usually, in fact, there's a long, embarrassing period of fiddling on your part—and fidgeting on the part of the audience.

Therefore, begin your opening remarks *immediately*, with the mike held in your hand, as we'll be discussing in the next chapter. After a moment or two—ideally during a laugh—you can *then* hang the mike around your neck, *without interrupting the flow of your speech*.

These are all small points. But they make an enormous difference. Once again, they add up to the kind of Miracle Platform Power that this book will help you develop.

Platform-Powered Introductions

The final factor in your Miracle Platform Power environment is the way you're introduced by the program chairman. Again, this can greatly affect the manner in which you're received by the audience.

So, as I've been suggesting right along, *you* tell the emcee how you want this done.

First, don't let the intro run too long. If you were going to type it on a single sheet of paper, that would be about as long as the first chapter of Genesis—which covered the entire creation of the heavens and the earth. This should be long enough to introduce you or me!

Second, don't let it go into too many vital statistics: "Our speaker was born in East Armpit, went to East Armpit High School, now lives in West Armpit." Who cares!

Third, don't let the chairman steal your stuff. You're the featured speaker. He isn't.

Instead, simply instruct the program chairman to tell the audience:

1) What the subject is;
2) Why it's important to the audience; and
3) Why *you're* qualified to talk about it.

In short, let the chairman tell the folks they're in for a real treat.

Then all *you* have to do is prove it!

Which, again, is what Miracle Platform Power is designed to help you do.

One subject that professional speakers often debate is: Should you have your introduction written out in advance, so the program chairman can read it verbatim?

Actually, there are good reasons *for* planning it this way—and equally good reasons for *not*.

If you luck into a topnotch chairman, he won't need a word-for-word intro. If you get stuck with a real loser, he may louse it up anyway. (It's astounding how many otherwise-capable people can't read!)

But, most of the pros on the circuit agree that having one ready is good insurance. (And, of course, if you use the Piggy-Back Opening which we'll be talking about in the next chapter, it's mandatory.) Anyway, on balance, a typewritten introduction generally helps more than it hurts.

Rolland Storey, a leading spokesman for the American free-enterprise system, suggests mailing your introduction to the chairman in advance *and* having an extra copy with you when you arrive. This way, you're saved even if the guy loses the mailed copy.

Rolland also makes a point of having his introduction typed out in *large jumbo letters.* As he puts it, "Program chairmen generally read better when they can see what they're reading!"

Summing all this up, you'll never be *guaranteed* a perfect introduction, no matter what you do. It's still up to the chairman as to how it all comes out—which, to some extent, puts it in the lap of God.

But you can *affect* the outcome by your own actions.

The introduction is an integral part of your Miracle Platform Power environment—and that makes it vitally important.

MIRACLE PLATFORM POWER CAPSULE

1) Your Platform Power environment is crucial:
   And it's your responsibility.

2) It's easy to get an SRO audience:
   Just don't give 'em too many places to sit down!

3) Capitalize on your audience's "herd-instinct" psychology:
   Keep 'em close to each other—and to you.

4) Get rid of head tables:
   They're for eaters, not for speakers.

5) Control temperature and lighting:
   Keep it cool—keep it bright.

6) Use the right mike:
   Let it be a help, not a hindrance.

7) Insist on a strong introduction:
   Have it highlight the subject, the audience, and you.

5

Creating Instant
Platform Power

Those All-Important First 10 Seconds

It's an old axiom in selling that the most critical period in any sales presentation is the first 10 seconds. That's when the prospect decides whether to listen to your story or turn you off completely. The same holds true in public speaking—doubled in spades.

During that first moment when you stand up to talk, the audience gains an instant impression, favorable or unfavorable, that largely determines the success of your entire speech. They're all immediately thinking to themselves (perhaps without realizing it): "I like this guy" or "He's a jerk" . . . "He's on top of the situation" or "He doesn't know what the hell he's doing" . . . "I want to hear this" or "I wish I could duck out to the bar." So, again, your opening is *critical*.

59

Your first job—as in selling—is to get them to like *you*. (More about this in Chapter 9.) Then they'll be in a far better mood to hear and enjoy what you have to say.

Admittedly, this can be a little tough on a speaker, because the audience usually doesn't know in advance what a great, lovable guy you really are! Bob Hope or Johnny Carson can come out and get thunderous applause just by being there—because the audience already *knows* them. You and I rarely have that luxury.

As speakers, *we* have to earn the audience's friendship by how we behave *after* we're introduced. And we have to do it *fast*.

That's why those first 10 seconds are *critical*.

Your Platform-Powered Appearance

It's a big help, of course, if you just naturally happen to *look* like a good guy. Among my fellow pros on the circuit, for instance, Herb True, Heartsill Wilson and Bill Gove come instantly to mind. These fellows (among many others) *are* great guys—off stage as well as on—and it *comes across instantly*.

But, even if you weren't born with the face of a movie star, at least you can be well *groomed*. This may seem terribly obvious, but it's another cardinal rule that's often violated.

My public speaking prof at Dartmouth used to say: "Be at least as well-dressed as the *best-dressed* person in your audience. Then you can't go wrong."

This means that if *anyone* is going to be in black-tie, you'd better have a tux on. If the majority are wearing sport jackets, with perhaps one or two business suits sprinkled through the audience, then *you* should be wearing a suit. And if it's a casual affair at a resort, where open-neck shirts are the standard attire, then *you* should have on a tie and sport coat.

Frankly, I inadvertently violated this rule myself once, and I regretted it.

The occasion was a sales meeting for Continental Oil Company, held at the lovely Grand Hotel in Point Clear, Alabama. Since that is a casual (though absolutely first-rate) resort, the company decided that *everyone* would wear sport shirts throughout the affair. As usual in such cases, I still held out and appeared in coat and tie. That was the *first* day. But then, in response to the urging—and gentle chiding—of the company management present, the *second* day I gave in and wore a long-sleeve sport shirt.

But *that* day the Conoco Vice-President, Tom Sigler, flew in for an appearance—and *he* was decked out in a well-tailored navy-blue business suit! So I was *not* , by any means, as well-dressed as the best-dressed man there—and it bothered me. (Since then, Conoco has hired me for other meetings, so I guess it wasn't all that bad. But, as I say, it bothered *me*.)

And that, of course, is the critical point. You have to *feel* confident to *look* confident.

So, let me give you a few other professional tips in this regard:

1) *Dress conservatively.* Wear subdued colors and patterns. You want them to concentrate on *you*, not your clothes. The great humorist, Jerry Clower, often wears a bright gold suit—and it ideally fits his style of comedy—but that's an exception. Normally, conservative clothes are decidedly best.

2) *Wear suspenders, not a belt.* Suspenders are rare in this casual age, but it's a proven fact that they allow your trousers to hang more smoothly and, hence, give you a better overall appearance.

3) *Check your zipper just before you go on.* (I said some of this may sound obvious!) But the fact is that you'll worry about it if you don't. And that's something you *don't* want to worry about!

My apologies to the ladies among my readers. The above tips were written from a male point of view. But the principles are still valid, and you can figure out how they apply to you.

The whole point is that you have to appear supremely confident without being overbearing—which, again, is why your total preparation is so crucial to your success. If you're *not* properly prepared, it's virtually impossible to fake it. If you are, it's pretty easy to project a self-confidence that's genuine.

And that, again, is why Miracle Platform Power means preparing *yourself* as well as your speech.

How to Warm Up for Greater Platform Power

Actually, you can give your opening a valuable head start by beginning even *before* you're introduced! How? Just by doing a few mental (or even physical) warm-ups immediately prior to your main entrance.

For instance, if you simply say to yourself, "I like these folks and they're going to like me," that's what will probably happen. Sure, it sounds corny—but it works.

Similarly, if you're not sitting at a head table in front of everybody (where this would admittedly look pretty silly), it's a good idea to practice a few smiles and grins to loosen up your facial muscles. In the same way, you can swing your arms and do a few in-place jogging steps to get the adrenalin flowing. Anything to get yourself in "high gear" for the actual opening itself.

The famous magician, Howard Thurston, was a master at this. He used to stand in the wings before every performance, jumping up and down and saying out loud: "I love my audience, I love my audience!" Yes, that was over a half-century ago, but it got the job done—and it still does. (I never *saw* this happen. I've only read about it!) Anyway, I know it works for me.

One word of caution in this regard.

It's a well known fact that some entertainers—and a few speakers—try to get themselves into a jovial mood by taking a few belts from a bottle just before going on. Don't! This can be suicide. (Just to keep the record straight, depending on the time of day, I do enjoy a drink or three *after* a performance. But *not before*.)

The fact is—repeating what I've been saying right along—your Miracle Platform Power depends on making it all *look* easy. But it still takes work. And that requires full concentration on the job at hand—concentration which even a minor amount of alcohol can destroy. So, the best rule is: Speak first; drink *later!*

Now, most (though clearly not all) of what I've been saying refers to what you can—or can't—do when you're actually in the wings, out of sight of your audience. How about a luncheon or dinner speech, where you're in full view of the audience before you begin? How can you go through your warm-ups in that situation?

As I said at the outset, you do it *mentally*. You make a conscious effort to *think* yourself ready—even to the extent of a silent re-rehearsal of your opening lines.

Another helpful hint is to survey the audience in front of you. Watch for those who seem to be in a good mood, the ones who smile and laugh easily—usually (though not always) the *leaders* in the crowd. Don't be afraid to look at them—even smile at them—and *let them smile back*.

Again, this is good *psychology*. Because, this way, you'll have some important *friends* in the audience—before you even begin! So, your opening itself is bound to be that much better received.

Bill Lufburrow is head of Goodwill Industries in Houston, an organization that is of tremendous benefit to the community. Always a strong and capable leader, Bill says that his *speaking* ability has become one of his greatest assets in building wide support for Goodwill's worthy efforts.

He excels—in front of service clubs and other groups everywhere—largely by *making friends* with his audiences. And he invariably warms up to his audiences *before* he gets up to talk— so they warm up to *him* the minute he starts to speak.

Once more, it's a technique that will surely create Miracle Platform Power for *you*.

Begin by Beginning

Okay, now that all of your preparation, rehearsal, and warm-up has been completed and the program chairman has concluded his introduction, what do you actually *say* during those critical first few moments?

Obviously, this is going to depend largely on the subject matter of your speech, the make-up of the audience, the affair as a whole, your own speaking style, and a lot of other factors.

But the essential rule is: *Begin by beginning*.

Some speakers feel compelled to open with a gag. I have no quarrel with this—and, in fact, normally do so myself—but only when it ties in with the subject matter *and* when useless preliminaries are avoided. So *don't* begin, as so many speakers do, by saying: "I don't usually tell jokes, but before I begin my speech I want to tell you one I heard the other day . . ." *Get on with it!*

Similarly, even though it's still customary at political conventions, *don't* start out with a recitation of all the dignitaries present: "Mr. Chairman, President Joe Doaks, Mrs. Doaks, distinguished guests at the head table, and ladies and gentlemen . . ."

Get on with it!

Also, don't begin with a cliché like: "Boy, after an introduction like that, I can't wait to hear what I've got to say . . ." *Get on with it!*

And, worst of all, don't start out with an apology: "Before I begin, let me tell you how I happened to be asked here . . ." or "I'm really not fully prepared, but I'll do my best . . ."or "I'm sorry I have a slight cold tonight . . ." "Can you hear me in the back?" and so forth.

Get on with it!

In the next section of this chapter, we'll analyze seven *good* ways to open. They're all different—but they have one crucial thing in common:

They all let you *begin by beginning*.

Seven Easy Ways to Immediate Audience Acceptance

Okay, here now are seven sure-fire ways to get any speech off to a strong beginning—to get audience psychology working for you right from the start:

1) **The Introducer-Builder Technique.** This is a way to capitalize on the *program chairman's* popularity to enhance your own. It truly builds immediate Platform Power—for the simple reason that whoever is called upon to introduce you is almost invariably already liked and respected by the audience.

At a recent meeting of the Houston Sales & Marketing Executives, for instance, the highly talented president of Stanley-Vidmar, Bill Devaney, was introduced by Park Myers, vice-president of Hughes Tool. As chairman of Sales & Marketing Executives International, Bill Devaney came with excellent credentials. But, *to the audience,* Park Myers, who did the introduction, was more of a known and beloved entity—particularly since the club had just awarded him a special plaque in recognition of his distinguished service to the organization.

So, what did Bill Devaney do? As a truly superb speaker, he *capitalized* on this by opening with *his own* congratulations for Park Myers!

That's using the Introducer-Builder Technique!

2) The Piggy-Back Opening. This is somewhat of a corollary to the above. It means using the *introduction* itself as a tie-in to your own opening remarks.

As an example, my good friend Jim Gillie, of Phillips Petroleum, addresses associations and other groups throughout the country. And he does so superbly. His prepared introduction, given to the program chairman in advance, recounts his many successes and accomplishments, and then says: "Despite all this, Jim Gillie is a very *humble* man." Whereupon Jim gets up and says: "I don't know where the heck you got that introduction, but you've got some nerve calling a guy from Phillips Petroleum a 'Humble' man!"

Now that the former Humble Oil Company has become Exxon, Jim has had to change this opening. Which he has. But the principle is still valid: It's how a pro uses the Piggy-Back Opening for immediate audience acceptance.

3)The Disclaimer. In no way an apology, this is simply a way to let the audience know that you're not going to "pressure" them into anything.

An excellent example of this is the fine talks made by Rollie McGinnis in behalf of the Public Broadcasting System. Rollie is a director of this worthwhile endeavor in Houston; he's also president of Higham's Cadillac Company. So, when addressing service clubs in behalf of public television, he begins by saying: "I'm not here to sell you a car—but merely to tell you about more enjoyable television."

Again, it's a way to get the audience *on your side from the start.*

4) The Self-Kidder Technique. This is without doubt one of the *best* ways to gain the immediate audience acceptance that's so important to the overall success of your speech. It simply means letting *yourself* be the butt of your opening remark.

The great Red Motley, chairman of the board of Parade Publications, often opens with this line: "I'm delighted to be here. Hell, at my age, I'm delighted to be anywhere!"

Bill Gove sometimes begins by talking about taking "memory courses"—and then (on purpose) mispronounces the chairman's name. Again, he makes *himself* the butt of the joke—and, hence, gets the audience on his side right from the start.

Zenn Kaufman, leading New York sales consultant, uses the Self-Kidder to gain favorable audience acceptance even *before* he stands up to talk. He provides the chairman with an impressive written introduction, and then—during its height—Zenn holds up a cardboard sign with three words inscribed on it: "I WROTE THIS!" It always gets a big laugh.

In my own case, I often "step out of the screen" following a showing of my Dartnell film. So I begin by saying: "Isn't it great to be a sex symbol!" It's obviously a Self-Kidder—and the audience invariably responds favorably.

5) The Reverse-English Opening. This is where you do a complete about-face. Admittedly, for good reason, it means conning your audience completely.

The best exponent of this technique, in my judgment, is the nationally-known sales trainer, Alan Cimberg. Frankly, the first time I heard Alan speak, he had me fooled completely.

Alan Cimberg—who is billed as (and is) a highly dynamic speaker—begins by *reading* a brief dissertation on salesmanship. It's awful! Then, suddenly, he throws down the written text and literally *bursts* across the stage. The audience is taken totally by surprise—and Alan is off to another great performance.

6) The Silent Opening. There's only one famous practitioner of this technique to my knowledge, and that's Chris Hegarty. But, undoubtedly, others can use it as well. It sure works miracles for Chris.

When Chris Hegarty is introduced, he often stands—smiling but totally immobile—silently before the audience. And he stands there *for a full minute!* It's a long time! Invariably, the audience gets restless. Sometimes the silence is broken by nervous chuckles, sometimes by applause—but always by anticipation.

Then—and only then—Chris begins with a comment that relates directly to his silent opening. Again, he gets the audience *on his side*.

7)The Provocative Statement. If none of the above openings fit your style, the safest bet is simply to begin with a strong statement alerting the audience to the subject matter you intend to discuss.

If you're giving a talk on estate planning, for example, you might open by saying: "Do you know what will happen to your wife if you never get home from this meeting tonight?" That'll grab 'em!

Similarly, my late sales training colleague, Elmer Wheeler, used to begin simply: "What makes people buy?"

So there you have seven distinct ways to create instant Platform Power.

They all get your speech off to a strong start. They all get audience psychology working for you the minute you stand up to talk.

One final word:

Whatever you say during those first few seconds on the platform, this is one part of your speech that *must* be memorized and rehearsed, for two reasons:

1) It's too important to leave to chance.

2) Knowing your opening, and knowing that you know it, will give you that extra measure of self-confidence that you need so desperately right at this moment.

Get the audience with you at the start, and the rest is downhill all the way.

MIRACLE PLATFORM POWER CAPSULE

1) Grab your audience during the first 10 seconds:
   Lose 'em then, and you'll never get 'em back.

2) Check your appearance:
   You have to look your best to be at your best.

3) Always warm up before you begin:
   This gives you a running start.

4) Leave out the preliminaries:
   The best way to begin is by beginning.

5) There are 7 easy ways to immediate audience acceptance:
   Use whichever method works best for you.

6

The Psychology
of Platform
Power Humor

When to Be Funny—And When Not To

Many speakers assume that humor is a necessary ingredient in any speech. It isn't. But it can be a tremendous assist—if applied properly.

The talks which are best remembered and most widely applauded, are almost always sprinkled with liberal doses of humor. So, if you want to be really effective as a public speaker, you'd better let your audiences laugh while they listen.

But not all the time!

There is, after all, a marked distinction between a humorous speaker (or humorist)—which is what we're talking about here—

and a comedian. The difference is that as speakers, you and I are there to deliver a *message*—and humor is a *means* toward that end—whereas the comedian's *sole* job is one of *entertainment*.

It is interesting to note that top-name comedians, too—Bob Hope and Red Skelton, for example—often close their shows on a serious note (an appeal to some charity, or whatever).

In any event, the prime consideration is the *purpose* of your talk, and the audience you'll be addressing. If you're going to be discussing the latest trends in embalming fluids, any humor might be out of place. (Or maybe not. I remember I once spoke at the Casket Manufacturers Convention, and was advised by the committee that the only jokes they preferred not to hear were those regarding "digging for business.")

Another factor, of course, is your own personality. Some people are just naturally funnier than others. Among the very top pros on the circuit, for example, Dr. Charles Jarvis is an absolute riot offstage as well as on. It's a virtual impossibility for him *not* to be funny! (Although, in line with what we're talking about here, he always delivers a strong message as well.) If you happen to have that inborn gift to make people laugh, maybe you can skip this chapter.

But, it's also a fact that comedy is a serious business. It must be studied, practiced and perfected. Johnny Carson admits that as a youngster he was extremely shy and introverted. He learned later *how* to be funny.

Getting back to the "when" of humor, the previous chapter suggests that the right kind of gag can be very helpful during your *opening*.

The late Bennett Cerf, for instance—always a top draw on the lecture circuit—sometimes used to begin by saying: "With an introduction like that, you wonder who they're talking about—sometimes people make mistakes. Like at the Academy Award Dinner in Hollywood last year, a fellow got up and introduced Jayne Mansfield—and it turned out to be two Yul Brynners!" That's a great line! (Though, unfortunately, no longer timely.)

Also, of course, you can sprinkle gags *during* your talk. (More about this later.) It's a mistake to assume that if you open with a joke, the rest of your message is so solemn that humor has no place in it. (Unless, of course, you're addressing the United Nations.)

But *don't* assume, either, that every line of your speech has to have a laugh built into it. Sometimes, at a climactic moment, humor can *destroy* the very point you're trying to make!

As for your ending—which is fully covered in Chapter 10—I personally feel that this is *not* the place for humor. Sure, George M. Cohan used to say, "Always leave 'em laughing"—but, again, he was an entertainer. For a speaker, it seems to me, it's far more important to leave 'em *thinking* and *doing*.

An excellent example of this point is our own 13-week Selling Aces Workshop, which has trained salesmen for companies like General Electric, Consolidated Edison, Oxford Paper, Eli Lilly Drug, and thousands of others.

During the final session of the course, everyone gives a talk titled "Forecasting My Future"—describing the new goals he has set for himself as a result of his attendance in the program. This is the last exercise in the entire course—except that initially we injected one brief humorous stunt *after* it, just as the folks were leaving the room.

That was a mistake!

After a few years, we found that the talks given by our students at that final session were so inspiring and compelling—and the response by the rest of the group always so strong (we've even had tears shed!)—that the humorous stunt which followed had a decidedly *negative* effect. So we dropped it!

The point is: *Use humor—but don't let it use you!*

Three Cardinal Rules for More Effective Humor

Here, now, are three simple tips to remember for more laughs—and more applause:

1) **The joke must make a point.** As I've been suggesting all along, your primary job is to convey a message. So, don't use the latest thigh-slapper from Playboy unless you can make it fit.

Sometimes, this just means a little more of the preparation

and rehearsal we talked about in Chapter 2, Also, in the Ready-Reference Story-Teller's Guide at the end of this book, you'll find the jokes listed by category. These are all audience-tested gags which can apply to many situations.

Dave Yoho, for instance, is one of the funniest guys on the circuit. He's a truly great story-teller. But he uses his humor to make a point. By doing so, his message becomes far stronger—*and the jokes themselves become much funnier!*

2) At the same time, it must be funny. There's nothing worse than an un-funny joke. And the longer a joke takes to tell, the more time you devote to it, the funnier it has to be. If a one-liner doesn't go over too well, you can keep right on going and hardly anybody notices; but after a big build-up, if the punch line brings only vacant stares, the silence can be deadly!

This is why it's safest to use the kind of sure-fire gags you'll find in the Ready-Reference Story-Teller's Guide. But, even so, the acid test is how *your* audiences react when *you* tell any given joke.

As I've said from the outset, this whole book is written with the *audience* in mind. *Your* audience. So listen to *them!* If *you* think a joke is funny, it *may* be. But if your audience *doesn't* think so, it *isn't!*

In making presentations on resort land development, George Schrader formerly told the jokes *he* liked best—and usually received a so-so response. Now he uses the gags his *audiences* laugh at—and his Platform Power has skyrocketed. The difference is truly a miracle!

3) Keep it clean. Over a back-room poker game, maybe anything goes. But not in front of an audience. So be sure to use humor that entertains—not material that offends.

Now, admittedly, the limitations today aren't as strict as they used to be. Even daytime television is full of double-entendres. So slightly risqué humor rarely bothers anyone. But there's a huge difference between jokes that are "cute" and those that are just plain vulgar.

One of the top stars in the entertainment industry once presented a full-evening show in Houston. During his opening, he said: "A lot of people think I talk dirty. That's a bunch of __ __ __ __." To me, that's plain vulgarity.

I saw a superb example of the fine—but clearly marked—line between "cuteness" and "dirtiness" recently at a Speakers Showcase staged in Atlanta.

Among the stars of the show, one of the most entertaining was Roy Hatten, who combines magic tricks with his humor—along with a strong message.

At one point in his presentation, a cane suddenly appears out of thin air. Roy goes on to show how the cane is really a coil of spring steel, kept in his trouser pocket and then later brought out and the catch released, which allows the thing to instantly expand. (Again, he does all this to prove a point in his talk—but it's not the one I'm trying to make here.)

My point is that Roy then relates how the catch on the device once accidentally released in his trouser pocket—and the thing suddenly expanded *there*. Everyone gets the picture—and laughs. *That*, to me, is *funny*.

But, on the same program, one not-so-pro tried for a similar laugh by unzipping his pants and pulling his shirt-tail straight out of his fly. *That*, to me, is *crude*.

Again, there's a line—and, as a speaker, it's up to you to stay within it.

Remember the rule: *If in doubt, leave it out.*

NOTE: One thing a joke *doesn't* have to be is *new*. Some of my colleagues may disagree with this, and, admittedly, if you can make your humor fit the *time* as well as the place, so much the better.

But, some of the very funniest stuff has been around for years. Even Will Rogers' lines, as presented by James Whitmore in his marvelous one-man shows on stage and TV, are as clever today as they were a couple of generations ago.

So, if the joke makes a point, if it's funny, if it's clean, and if you tell it well, go ahead and use it.

Even if it's the oldest gag in the world, you'll find that 90% of your listeners have never heard it.

How to Tell Jokes Funny, Not Funny Jokes

As suggested in the previous section of this chapter, you have to pick the right gag to start with. If the joke just plain isn't funny, no audience is going to laugh.

But, still, you also have to *tell it properly* if you want it to really go over.

Here are 4 ways to make your jokes funnier:

1) Keep it short. Leave out all the excess garbage. Don't "narrate" a gag. *Tell* it!

We've all heard jokes that sound like this: "It seems there were these two guys in a bar . . . and well, you know, things were kinda busy that evening . . . it was Saturday night, or something like that . . . and, see, this cat comes in—or maybe it was a dog . . . let's see if I can remember . . ." and so on and so on.

Do *you* laugh at that sort of thing? Neither will your audience!

There are, of course, *raconteurs*—Myron Cohen, for instance—who build humor *into* a joke by drawing it out. But not many.

The safest bet is to stick to the old adage: "Brevity is the soul of wit."

2) Know it word for word. The only way to follow the first rule is to have the joke down *pat*.

Once again, this means preparation and *rehearsal*. And it also means following the In/Out Step we talked about way back in Chapter 2, It's the only way to make sure your gags come out the way you want them to—smoothly and with precision.

And when you rehearse your gags, also rehearse the *pauses*. Usually there should be only *one* pause in each joke—just before the punch line. Nowhere else.

For example, in talking about the importance of time, one of my own favorite lines goes like this:

"Things do take time. I remember back in World War II, they gave us these little pills to stop thinking about girls . . . I'm finding out now they're just beginning to work!"

And that's the way it *sounds*—with the pause precisely where I've indicated. (Also note that this is my definition of a "cute" joke, not a dirty one.)

Again, to get the laugh you want, the line must be delivered right on the money.

3) Leave something to the imagination. Give your listeners credit for their intelligence. Let them feel that *they're* as clever as you are!

One of the biggest laughs that Jack Benny ever got in his entire career was on radio, when a robber stopped him on the street and demanded, "Your money or your life!" There was a long pause of dead air. The robber repeated, "I said your money or your life!" Whereupon Benny finally answered, "I'm thinking, I'm thinking!"

Jack Benny did *not*, you'll notice, say: "Well, I'll have to decide whether I'd rather have my money or my life." At first, he said *nothing*. And then only: "I'm thinking, I'm thinking!"

Giving *you* credit for *your* intelligence, you get my point.

4) Make yourself the goat. Whenever possible, let the audience laugh at *you* a little. They'll like you better for it!

Talking about Jack Benny, he was an absolute master at this. So is Bob Hope. Again, there are exceptions—like Don Rickles— but usually, if you're going to make somebody the goat, it's safer to let that somebody be yourself.

For instance, the first time I heard the one about the "little pills back in World War II," it was used by a speaker on somebody *else*. He said to a member of the *audience:* "I'll bet you remember those little pills . . ." Frankly, I think it's funnier my way.

In Chapter 9, we'll be talking about other techniques to get the audience to *like* you better. Which is what audience psychology is all about.

But, for now, one of the best ways to tell jokes funny—and not just tell funny jokes — is to let yourself be the goat.

Once again, it's good *psychology*.

And, hence, it makes for greater Platform Power.

How to Keep 'Em Laughing After the Joke Is Over

Laughter is like applause: The longer it lasts, the better it becomes—for the speaker *and* for the audience.

So it's important to practice and rehearse what you're going to say and do *after* the joke as well as during it.

Some speakers, of course, say and do nothing. They just deadpan it. The late Herb Shriner, for instance, did this; it was his style. But, for most of us, this is *not* the best procedure.

Other speakers actually *frown* after every gag. To me, that says to the audience: "That joke wasn't very funny, was it?" So this, as far as I'm concerned, is totally wrong.

Another thing to avoid is a nervous chuckle. This, too, is *bad* psychology.

Some top performers—Al Capp and Sam Levenson, for example—do laugh out loud *during* a joke, and sometimes following it. But they do this with genuine amusement—actually enjoying it themselves.

The safest bet is to do what Bob Hope does: simply stand there and *smile*, for however long the laugh lasts. This communicates true humor in two directions—between you *and* the audience—which, of course, is the ideal kind.

But the *best* way to build the laugh following a joke is to *repeat the straight line*.

Kirk Kirkpatrick, another platform pro, uses this gag in connection with the point that you can't be first at everything:

"George Washington was first in war, first in peace, and first in the hearts of his countrymen. And he was the first President of the United States . . . But he married a widow!"

And then Kirk follows this by repeating: "You can't be first at everything!"

This way, the laugh is extended—and the point is further reinforced.

Frankly, this same technique has helped build my own Miracle Platform Power over the years.

It can do the same for you.

How to Make 'Em Laugh When They Don't

This is probably the toughest section in the book to write. Because when you tell a joke—and the folks know they're supposed to laugh at it—it's mighty tough when they don't!

But, still, it's right at this point that the pros are separated from the amateurs. You can win 'em or lose 'em—then and there.

The amateur just "gives up." He decides to himself (consciously or unconsciously): "To hell with it!" And his speech goes down the tube.

Some nightclub comics have been known to blame the audience. They rap on the mike, pretending it's not on. Or they say: "I know you're out there; I can hear you breathing!"

Wrong! It's *your* job to win over the audience, not the other way around.

So the only *right* thing to do in this situation is to keep your cool—and *stay in there*.

To my mind, Johnny Carson is—without question—the greatest in the world in this regard. In his job, he *has* to come up with new stuff every night (even though he obviously has top writers to help him). It can't *all* be that funny. A lot of it isn't.

But he *stays in there*.

In many cases, he has prepared "ad libs" to follow the gags that don't go over. He may kid with the audience about the response he did or didn't get. Or he just follows up a bad gag with a good one. In any case, *"the show goes on."*

These are good points for all of us to remember.

Let's face it, audiences do vary. Some are more responsive than others. Some of this, you have control over (see Chapter 4); some of it, you don't. And when the audience is better, *you* are better. We all are!

But the reverse is equally true: When *you* are better, *the audience is better!*

Bill Gove makes the point that he is never responsible *for* his audiences. But, as he puts it: "I am always responsible *to* my audiences!"

Amen.

Platform Power means doing the very *best* possible job in *every* situation, with *every* audience.

MIRACLE PLATFORM POWER CAPSULE

1) People like to laugh while they listen:
   But they also want to hear a message.

2) Remember the three rules for better humor:
   Make it fit; make it funny; keep it clean.

3) Don't just tell funny jokes, tell jokes funny:
   The laugh depends on you.

4) Know what to say and do following a gag:
   Keep 'em laughing after the joke is over.

5) Every audience can be won over:
   With some, you just have to try harder.

7

Building Miracle Platform Power Through Showmanship

How Showmanship Can Destroy Your Platform Power

Showmanship in a speech is a lot like humor (which, of course, we talked about in the previous chapter). It can be a tremendous assist if used properly—or, if misused, it can louse you up completely.

First, let's agree that showmanship *does* have a place in any talk you give. For, as speakers, you and I are "performers." Certainly not in the sense of being con men or sideshow barkers, but merely in the sense that we want to apply all the techniques we can to add luster to every presentation. This is why I've emphasized *professionalism* throughout the book.

And as with humor, showmanship is a valuable means toward that end.

But, it is *not* the end in itself. The real end, *always*, is the message itself, and how it's perceived by the audience.

What I'm suggesting, very simply, is that any showmanship that *adds* is good. Any that *detracts* is bad.

As an example, Zig Ziglar, another top headliner on the platform, makes a point of running all over the stage, and often crouching low with knees bent almost double, before springing up again.

Now with Zig, this is superb showmanship. He happens to be a very trim and graceful guy. So all this physical action decidedly increases his Platform Power and, hence, it's excellent audience psychology—especially since part of his message involves the importance of keeping fit. On Zig, it looks great!

But, I've seen other speakers—far less agile than Zig Ziglar—try this same form of showmanship and fail to achieve equal results. In one case I can think of, the only reaction on the part of the audience was one of fear that the poor guy would fall over! So, in that instance, the showmanship didn't add, it *detracted*!

In discussing their forthcoming annual Sales Rally, the Executive Director of the Sales & Marketing Executives Association said to me recently, "I sure hope you can give the folks some *tangible ideas* of lasting benefit, not just an evening of entertainment."

He continued, "The guy we had last year did a pretty good job—until he ended by doing a song-and-dance act up the aisle, complete with straw hat and cane! And that *turned everybody off!*"

The showmanship didn't help, it *hurt*!

In my own case, as I've said, I started as a professional magician—and I was pretty good at it. (I'm probably the only man you know who was held over in Hawthorne, Nevada!) So, quite logically, when I began on the speaking circuit some 25 years ago, I sprinkled my talks with lots of magic tricks. I thought it would be great showmanship.

I was dead wrong! I found that the tricks *detracted* more from each speech than they *added* to it! Why? Simply because I tried to let the magic be an end in itself—rather than the *means* toward the end.

Note: I still inject a very *few* tricks into my presentations. In fact, in my Dartnell film, "Sell Like an Ace, Live Like a King," the script (which I didn't write) called on me to deal out certain winning and losing poker hands—so, here the sleight-of-hand had a definite place.

And that, of course, is the whole point I'm trying to make: Magic (or any other kind of showmanship) is great if it *fits*. It's very *bad* if it doesn't. And that, too, is why Roy Hatten's magic goes over so well, as I mentioned in Chapter 6: Not only is it *performed* expertly, but it's used to make a *point*.

One more example of what I'm talking about:

As I've already mentioned, one of the very *best* showmen on the American platform is Herb True. In fact, he's billed as "The World's Greatest Edu-tainer"—meaning that he's part educator and part entertainer. And that he is! No question.

But at a recent meeting of the select Professional Sales Trainers Group (membership as of this writing, alphabetically: Alan Cimberg, Don Hutson, Herb True, Heartsill Wilson, John Wolfe, Dave Yoho), Herb told the rest of us that he's *changed* some of his showmanship in recent years.

Formerly, Herb appeared in a variety of different costumes: doctor, prison inmate, pirate, etc. His costumes were important props in his presentations.

But now, Herb says, he's dropped the special costumes—simply because he's found that audiences are more interested in hearing what he has to *say* than they are in looking at a comic costume!

Again, paralleling the case of humor, use showmanship—but don't let it use you.

Kevin O'Sullivan, executive director of the American Society for Training and Development, sums it up this way: "Sure, people like to be entertained. But they also want *information*—something they can take away and *use*."

For real Miracle Platform Power, the *message* is what counts.

Planning for Platform-Powered Showmanship

As I've been saying, showmanship can be a huge asset in any speech, as long as it adds to—and doesn't detract from—the message you're there to get across.

And, as with every other phase of your presentation, the showmanship you inject must be *planned* and *rehearsed*.

In the planning stage, here are three tips to keep in mind:

1) Make it unique. The effectiveness of your showmanship depends wholly on the impact it makes on the audience. And that, in turn, depends largely on the element of *surprise*.

Thom Norman, for instance, is a leading pro in the field of telephone selling. In his appearances around the country, Thom makes actual, bona fide telephone appointments—right in front of the audience—to people he has never met. He *proves* his methods work by using them right there on the stage! Talk about putting yourself on the line!

This is tremendously effective because it's *different*. And if some of the folks may know in advance that this is going to be part of Thom's presentation, there is still a huge element of *surprise*. Even Thom has no way of knowing exactly how each call will turn out!

When you think of it, this provides a little of the same sort of suspense that Houdini used to build up before his famous escape act. You knew Houdini was going to try to escape from, say, a block of ice. You *didn't* know for sure that he'd succeed!

Another example of this surprise factor in showmanship is a stunt often used by H. B. "Doc" Sharer, one of the all-time greats on the platform until he retired a few years ago.

Doc would relate, at some length, how a smart young salesman sold him a shirt by emphasizing the long-lasting qualities of the collar, the cuffs, and the buttons. And that, Doc would go on to say, is why he bought the shirt.

And then came Doc's surprise punch line: "The only thing he *didn't* tell me is how long the *rest* of the shirt would last!"

At which point Doc would jump up on a chair and rip off his coat—showing a torn shirt full of gaping holes!

Again, the element of surprise.

2) **Keep it simple.** Some speakers try to overwhelm their audiences by the sheer volume of stuff they tote around with them. This is unnecessary—and, once more, puts you in danger of letting your props overshadow the message.

Rolland Storey, for instance, once made up a gigantic "Blast Furnace Sales Machine" to show how sales were made. The contraption was nine feet high and weighed 4000 pounds! It was clever as the dickens! But it was also a terrible nuisance!

Now, instead, Rolland closes his inspiring talks with a recorded song about "Americanism." He finds there's a far greater impact—and, at the same time, far less gimmickry. And it keeps the spotlight on *Rolland* instead of on his props!

In my own case, I used to display my special "Selling Aces" cards on a custom-made wooden easel. At the top of the easel there was a tray to hold the five cards: "Before the Sale, Start with a Spade" . . . "In Every Approach, Hit 'Em in the Heart" . . . "When Demonstrating, Deal in Diamonds" . . . "To Clinch the Close, Cushion 'Em with a Club" . . . and "The Joker—Do It!"

Naturally, each of these large cards was brought out at the appropriate time and then placed in its proper position in the tray.

At the conclusion of the talk, I'd release a catch at the back of the easel, whereupon a sort of canvas "windowshade" device would unroll, displaying the legend: "With Plenty of Jack" . . . . "For You and Your Queen" . . . . "You'll Live Like a King" . . . . "If You Sell Like an Ace!"

Clever? Sure! But it was also too *complicated*.

Later, I had the special wooden hand constructed which I referred to several chapters ago. This way, the cards can be larger, the total impact is greater, the uniqueness is still there—and there's far less fiddling around.

Again, keep it simple.

3) Stay in style. We'll be talking more about speaking style in Chapter 9. But notice, in all the examples just given, that each showmanship stunt I've mentioned fit the individual style of the speaker.

Thom Norman is the only person I know who makes live telephone calls. Doc Sharer made the torn-shirt gag his trademark. Rolland Storey's "Americanism" recording was orchestrated especially for him. The "Selling Aces" are copyrighted in my own name.

But, even simpler forms of showmanship can become part of your own personality. If they don't, in fact, they shouldn't be used.

Charles "Tremendous" Jones, for instance, is another top platform pro. One of his "trademarks" is the way he works with the audience—especially the front row.

He will run down to a guy in the front, yell at him eyeball-to-eyeball, and even slap him on the shoulder!

Now, this is his *style*. The way he does it, it's highly effective. In all candor, I would *not* feel comfortable doing this. I work with my audiences in *other* ways (see Chapter 9). But for Charlie, it's great showmanship. It fits his personality.

Ira Hayes also has a unique brand of showmanship. Ira is still another platform headliner, and his trademark is the multitude of different props he uses to illustrate his points. When Ira gets through with one of his dynamic presentations, the stage looks like a department store!

This, by the way, does *not* contradict my previous point about "keeping it simple." Ira's props are not complicated. There are just lots of them! And, they also fit his bubbling style.

So, once more: Make it unique; keep it simple; stay in style.

Now, obviously, no matter how carefully you plan your showmanship, it will never be perfect the *first time*. That's why you have to practice and rehearse and practice some more—and be ready to make changes when you find a better way.

A sweet young girl once said to the famous English Prime Minister, Benjamin Disraeli: "Oh, Mr. Disraeli, that was a marvelous impromptu speech you gave this afternoon." Disraeli answered: "My dear, I've been preparing that impromptu speech for twenty years!"

My own "Selling Aces" format was first introduced to the New York Sales Managers Club in 1956. I've changed it over the years, and much has evolved since that first "opening night." But, the basic concept has been putting groceries on the Wolfe family table ever since.

Mainly because it's *mine*.

I urge you, in every speech, to make sure that what you present is *yours*.

How To Use Visual Aids—Effectively

As you've undoubtedly noticed from all of these examples, showmanship should appeal to the *eyes* as well as the ears.

Once again, it's good *psychology*.

Psychologists say that we remember 1/5 of everything we hear, 2/5 of everything we see, and 4/5 of everything we *see and hear*.

So, if you want your audiences to remember what you've said to them—and, even more important, *to do something about it*—you'd better let 'em look while they listen.

So, now, let's talk about typical *visual* aids—which to use, and how best to use them:

1) **Blackboard.** This, of course, is what we all grew up with in school. (Now, since it may be green or blue, it's also referred to as a "chalkboard," but most people still call it a blackboard.)

It has three prime advantages: 1) It's highly flexible; 2) It's quick and easy to use; and 3) You can find one almost anywhere you're called upon to speak.

Its prime disadvantage is the very fact that it is so commonplace. It is by no means "sophisticated" compared to the electronic gadgetry most of us have in our own living rooms.

But for relatively small groups—say, no more than fifty—the blackboard is a highly useful, versatile tool.

TIPS: When you use a blackboard, keep it clean, well erased, so what you write on it can be clearly seen. For the same reason, write in *large block letters*—using the blunt edge of the chalk, so your strokes are *thick* enough as well as high enough.

Also, when using a blackboard, *don't stand in front of it*. Stand to the *side*, so the audience can see you *and* the message you're writing, at the same time that you're talking about it. If you're right-handed, have the board at *stage right*, so your arm doesn't get in the way.

2) **Flip Chart.** This is another common device, available at most hotels (or from any art supply store). It has a large pad of paper on which you can write with a special "marker" pen.

Its advantages are much the same as the blackboard's: It's quick and easy to use. Also, with the various colors of markers available, you can add more variety by writing your message in black, red, blue or whatever.

Another advantage of the flip chart: Since you have a whole pad of paper to work with, you can have certain messages written out on the back pages *in advance*, which you can then reveal at the appropriate times in your presentation.

Again, as with the blackboard, the flip chart's chief disadvantage is its limited visibility in front of large audiences.

But it's another valuable tool that can add important showmanship to your presentation.

TIPS: Limit the message on each page to a *very few words*. Don't try to put a full dissertation on any one. Also, don't let the marker lie open too long; it dries out and writes nothing—which isn't good showmanship at all!

3) **Flannel Board.** Now we get into some of the more sophisticated kinds of visuals. If you want real impact—still with versatility—the flannel board is an excellent device.

Essentially, as its name implies, the flannel board is a board (of whatever size) covered with a thick flannel-like material in black. Specially prepared cardboard signs are similarly backed with the same material. Then, when the board is placed on an easel at a slight incline the cardboard signs can be "slapped" onto the board at will, and they'll stay there until removed!

The essential advantage here, of course, is variety. The cardboard signs can be any size, any shape, any color. Also, there's more *professionalism* in the fact that the signs are necessarily done in advance and, hence, can be precisely lettered and designed.

So, if you have a presentation that you're going to be giving repeatedly—or even if it's *one* presentation that you want to carry real impact—the flannel board is an excellent device.

When Ford Motor Company used my own sales training program to train their dealers throughout the world, a flannel board presentation was one of the essential elements we used. So I know it works!

TIPS: As with the blackboard and flip chart, keep your flannel board at stage right (unless you're left-handed) so you don't get yourself in the way. Also, slap the cardboard signs on *smartly,* so they stay there without threatening to fall off, until you're ready to remove them.

4) **Velcro Board.** This is a device very similar to the flannel board. (It's also known as "Hook & Loop.") Actually, it's the same principle used in fastening certain garments. There's a large black board—like a flannel board only less "flannelly"—with a series of pre-designed cardboard signs, on the back of which you affix a special "gauze-like" material. Then, somehow, when each sign is placed against the board, it stays there.

Only this time (unlike with the flannel board) it *really* stays there! You have a heck of a time pulling it off!

And that's its *disadvantage* as well as its *advantage!* If you want to shuffle your signs around—put them on, take them off, etc.—the velcro board can present a problem.

But if you have just *one* display to put up, this is a great device. And the further advantage of the velcro board is that it can hold *other* objects as well—tools, parts or whatever. The hold is that strong!

TIPS: In using the velcro board, just a *small* piece of the gauze-like material on the back of your signs (or whatever) will do the job. Don't use more than is necessary.

5) **Overhead Projector.** This is an extremely common device among business educators. It allows a slide to be projected on a screen at the front of the room—and, again, allows great flexibility.

As usual, there are both advantages and disadvantages.

The big advantage over the other visual aids already discussed is that you can reach a larger audience. The screen can be virtually as large as you want it to be.

The main disadvantage is that you have to manipulate the projector each time you change a slide.

So, there are pros and cons.

TIPS: As I've been suggesting all along, don't let the visuals—in themselves—steal your stuff. *You* must remain the star. If necessary, bring along an assistant to change the slides as needed. This way, you can keep a separate spotlight zeroed in on *you*.

6) **Slide Projector.** Another common device used by many speakers. The Kodak "Carousel" is probably the most familiar example.

Here, you can get into a really first-rate professional presentation. The "professionalism," of course, depends on how well the slides are prepared and how expertly the entire production is put together.

Example: Keith Butler, National Advertising Manager of the Houston Post, has produced a fast-moving slide presentation—complete with sound and music—that is shown to major corporations and ad agencies everywhere. It's a real bang-up production. And it's made a world of difference in the Post's advertising lineage.

TIPS: As Keith Butler suggests, don't let any one slide remain on the screen more than a few seconds. Keep 'em short—and keep 'em moving!

7) **Movie.** A motion-picture film is, without doubt, the most graphic visual aid you can use.

For most speakers, the obvious disadvantage is that a movie is extremely expensive to produce. So, you may simply not be able to use this medium.

But, at the same time, if you *can* come up with a professional film you'll probably find it highly effective.

TIPS: Know what you're going to say before and after the film itself, so it ties in directly with your overall message. Make sure the projector is aimed at the screen and in proper focus before you begin. Have someone ready to switch off the lights on cue.

Clyde Beall, Special Services Supervisor of Houston Natural Gas, is an experienced pro in film presentation. He does it the right way! Mainly because of his meticulous attention to *details*.

For example, Clyde insists on having all exposed wires *taped to the floor,* so no one can trip on them and knock over his $800 projector!

As I've been suggesting all along, the key to Platform Power is *professionalism*.

And this probably applies to using showmanship more than anywhere else.

Five Audience-Tested, Off-Beat Stunts

There are, of course, zillions of gimmicks and gadgets you can use to liven up your presentations—several of which we've just been talking about. They may require a certain amount of preparation—and, in some cases, a certain amount of expense.

But, there are other *easy* ways to inject more showmanship into your speeches *without* extensive (or expensive) production costs.

Here are five:

1) **The YCMABSOYC Gag.** This is ideal for sales meetings. All you have to do is be willing to invest $1.00 in each of your salesmen.

Before the meeting begins—and before anyone is in the room—simply tape a dollar bill underneath the seat of each chair.

Then, conduct your meeting as usual, saying nothing (and giving no hint) as to the dollars under the chairs. They'll never be noticed!

During the meeting, of course, you'll be telling your people what to do and how to do it, or whatever else you intend to cover.

At the conclusion of the meeting, tell everyone to look under the seat of his or her chair. Everyone gets up to do so—and finds the dollar.

The moral, you point out, is: "*You Can't Make a Buck Sitting on Your Chair!*" (Note: You can make the initials YCMABSOY-A if you prefer.)

It's a great way to end a sales meeting!

2) Introductions. These work best when you're in front of an audience of strangers—meaning that the folks are strangers to *each other*, not just to you. (Obviously, it would *not* work at, say, a Rotary Club.)

During your opening remarks, you comment that you "should all get to know each other better" (or whatever similar phrase fits into your presentation.)

Whereupon you ask each person to introduce himself (or herself) to the person in the next seat, and shake hands.

It's amazing how this warms up an audience! They warm up to each other—and to *you*!

3) Backward Introductions. This is simply a twist on the above. Again, you need an audience of strangers—and you need an *auditorium-style* seating arrangement. (As you'll see, this *doesn't* work if folks are facing each other across tables.)

With this stunt, again as in the one above, you begin by emphasizing the importance of "getting to know people better."

Then, you say: "At the count of three, everyone please turn around and shake hands with the person in *back* of him. One . . . Two . . . Three!"

At which point the whole audience will turn around—and each person will be shaking hands with a bare back!

Again, it's a surprise, it gets a laugh—and you get a warmer audience!

4) The Numbers Game. This takes just a little preparation, but it's worth it. It's especially appropriate when one of your major points (in any context) is "knowing how to do the job."

Before the meeting, you need to prepare a sheet of paper (normally standard 8½" x 11" size) with sixty circles, each about the size of a penny, scattered throughout the sheet. In each of these circles you write a number—one through sixty—in apparently random fashion. At first glance, there's no rhyme or reason as to the specific placement of the numbers.

Then, all you have to do is run off enough copies of the sheet for the number of folks you'll have in your audience.

At the appropriate time, you pass out the sheets, telling everyone to keep them *face down* until you give the okay to turn them over.

You announce that there are sixty numbered circles on the page. You also say that the object of the exercise is to draw a line from circle 1 to circle 2, then to circle 3, next to circle 4, etc. And you point out that everyone must do this *as quickly as possible.* Time is of the essence!

Then, having explained these instructions, you say, "Go!" and everyone turns over his paper and begins.

At the end of, say, twenty seconds, you call "Time!" and everybody stops.

You then ask how many have finished, how many got past forty, thirty and so on. The results will be amazingly bad!

Now—and this is the whole point of the stunt—you tell everyone to *fold the paper lengthwise,* and you then ask if anyone notices anything about the placement of the numbers. *Immediately,* everyone will see that all the odd numbers are on one side of the sheet, and all the even numbers are on the other. (This, of course, is how you placed them.) But *no one* noticed it before!

The point, of course, is that if you know *how* to do something, the job becomes far easier!

And you can *prove* this by giving the folks another twenty seconds to continue drawing the lines from number to number—starting wherever they left off—invariably the results are vastly different!

Again, it's showmanship that makes a *point.*

5) The Instruction Quiz. This is another stunt requiring just a little advance preparation. But the audience reaction justifies it! It has to do, as its name implies, with "following instructions."

Again, you need to make up a special 8½" x 11" sheet. At the top you put: "*How Well Do You Follow Instructions?*" Below that, you list, say, twenty-five specific things to do — numbered 1 through 25.

Number 1 says: "Read everything on this page before doing anything."

Number 25 says: "Do Number 2 only."

And Number 2 says simply: "Write your name at the top of this sheet."

Then, Numbers 3 through 24 instruct the person to do *all kinds of crazy things*—which, of course, by virtue of the last item, the folks are not supposed to do at all!

One of the instructions, for instance, may be to circle your name; one may be to stand up and turn around before sitting down again; one may be to spell your last name backward—out loud. Etc., etc.

Again, you tell the folks they're being timed, that they have to hurry! And you keep the pressure on during the allotted period!

A very few people will follow the instructions given; will read through the entire list; and, hence, will say and do nothing except write their names.

The rest of the group will go crazy! They'll jump up and down, shout out inane things—and, in the end, feel pretty sheepish.

But you'll *get your point across!*

Naturally, this should be done with a genial air—especially at the end. You are, after all, "conning" the audience to some extent, and you don't want resentment. But handled properly, it's tremendously effective.

One of the best "in-house" sales trainers in the country is Les Willson of DuPont, and you ought to see the mileage *he* gets out of The Instruction Quiz!

So, there are five sure-fire off-beat stunts that you can use in a multitude of situations.

They all add strong impact to your Platform Power.

MIRACLE PLATFORM POWER CAPSULE

1) Showmanship can add Miracle Platform Power to any speech:
   Just don't let it get in your way.

2) Showmanship must be meticulously planned and rehearsed:
   Make it unique; keep it simple; stay in style.

3) Use the right visual aid—and use it properly:
   Let your audiences look while they listen.

4) Build your Platform Power through tested off-beat stunts:
   They're easy to use—and highly effective.

8

How Platform Power Avoids Pitfalls

Reversing Murphy's Law

We're all familiar with the age-old adage ascribed to a certain Mr. Murphy: "Anything that *can* go wrong, *will* go wrong."

It's certainly as true in public speaking as anywhere else. With all the pressures involved, perhaps more so.

And the results can be more devastating. Especially to your ego.

Say you're out in a rowboat, in the middle of a lake, and your fishhook comes loose. So what? You don't mind all that much, because you're all alone and nobody else is aware of your goof. But when you're up there on that platform and a few hundred pairs of eyes are staring at you, you could just *die!*

So, it's important to *reverse* Murphy's Law wherever possible.

How? Simply by making sure—at least as sure as possible—that nothing *can* go wrong.

Think back, if you will, over some of the examples already mentioned throughout the book:

Chapter 1: At that United Fund rally, when Sammy Davis made sure that his music and mikes and lights were all precisely orchestrated, he was *reversing Murphy's Law.*

Chapter 2: In my own "Topper and O'Leary" magic act, our endless rehearsals were designed solely to *reverse Murphy's Law.*

Chapter 3: The suggestion to stash your notes underneath the podium surface until you're ready to use them—again, *Murphy's Law reversed.*

Chapter 4: Rolland Storey uses the technique of always carrying a spare copy of his introduction along with him. This *reverses Murphy's Law.*

Chapter 7: Clyde Beall's insistence on having his projector power cord taped to the floor—once more, *Murphy's Law reversed.*

And many more.

Most of this book is aimed at helping you accomplish this one objective; reversing Murphy's Law.

Because, if you let him, "old Murph" can kill you.

The Key to Preparation

It's obvious from all of this that you can rarely correct your mistakes *after* they occur. You have to stop them in *advance.* This is why I've continually emphasized the importance of proper preparation.

This means thorough, minute attention to every detail—*before* you stand up to talk.

And, undoubtedly, the biggest single key to all this is: *Get there early.*

I remember the very first full-evening sales rally I did for a Sales and Marketing Executives group—way back in 1957.

The program was scheduled to begin at 8:00 P.M. The committee—good hosts that they were—insisted on taking me out for dinner. "Don't worry," they said. "We'll get you to the auditorium in plenty of time." And naive as I was in those days, I went along. The guys were well-intentioned, of course. But as it turned out, I was hustled through the stage door just moments before the curtain went up.

Never again!

So, here are the rules I follow:

1) Get to the meeting *room* an *hour* before the program begins. Note: This does not mean an hour before the speech; it means an hour before the entire *program*. All preparation must be concluded before the audience arrives.

2) Get to the *city* of the meeting at least *three hours* before the program begins. This way, there's time for a shower and change. If it's an afternoon or evening appearance, a morning flight works out fine. But if it's a morning or luncheon date, the only way to maintain your schedule is to arrive the evening before.

In fact, if I'm doing an all-day seminar right here in Houston, or even kicking off an early-morning meeting, I'll normally check into the hotel the previous evening. Sure, it costs the client a few bucks more, but it gives them a far better program than if I'd spent 45 minutes fighting rush-hour traffic.

Another corollary: When I check into a hotel, in any city, I do it *early* in the evening, before dinner if at all possible. Again, this is just so I can be at my best the next day.

These are just *my* rules. But most of my colleagues on the circuit follow the same procedures. So should you.

Admittedly, it's not always possible for any of us to schedule things exactly the way we'd like.

Cavett Robert, one of the very busiest of the pros—and surely one of the best—likes to tell about the time he spoke at a breakfast in Boston and at another breakfast in San Francisco—on the same day! That's cutting it close!

In my own case, I conducted an afternoon seminar for Grumman American Aviation in Frankfurt, West Germany, on a Thursday; caught a Lufthansa flight back to Chicago on Friday; made a connection to Akron the same evening; checked into the motel there at 7:00 P.M. (which was *2:00 A.M.* according to the time I'd gotten up that morning) and then did a full-day seminar there on Saturday!

That's show biz!

But, still, it's far better to get there early.

How Jack Morton Does It

One of the very finest industrial show producers in America is Jack Morton Productions—headquartered in Washington, D.C., with other offices throughout the country.

As it happens, they were in charge of the audio-visual work for the Grumman American Aviation meeting in Germany which I just mentioned. During the preceding two weeks, working with them, I did three other Grumman American seminars in Tampa, Tulsa and Las Vegas. So I was able to observe these highly professional people in action.

First, they had at least two trained technicians at each location to handle the staging, projection equipment and so forth. At the first meeting, their Atlanta manager, Jerry Suit, was also on hand to supervise.

All of these people were at the respective hotels *two days early*. This way, everything was set up—stage, rear-screen projectors, room decorations and so on—during the day before the meeting.

The point is, *nothing was left to chance*. So, Murphy's Law was not only reversed—it was repealed!

Again, the point is obvious. You may never be able to commandeer two or three assistants to help you set up your materials on both sides of the Atlantic, a couple of days early. You may never need to. But the Jack Morton people are pros—and that's why their services are in demand. The closer you come to this kind of professionalism, the greater your Platform Power. Or, to put it another way, the early bird gets the applause.

Four Things to Do When Something Does Go Wrong

So far in this chapter, we've been concentrating on how to *prevent* goofs. Now let's talk about how to *cope* with them when they do occur. As they will!

Because, let's face it, neither you nor I will ever achieve perfection. Babe Ruth is remembered for his home runs, but he also piled up the greatest strike-out record in history!

Here are the four best ways to handle the situation when things go wrong:

1) **Have an out and use it.** Obviously, this also requires some advance planning. But, again, it's worth it.

I'm reminded of the time when I flew an 85 horsepower, single-engine (no radio) Taylorcraft from Mexico to Cuba. The distance was 160 miles over the ocean, navigating solely by dead reckoning. Why not? Lindbergh made it to Paris.

Except that *my* navigation, honest, had to be more on the money than his did. Aiming at the pointed end of Cuba, I had only a five-degree margin of error. Off more than that in either direction and I'd miss the island completely.

But here was my out: Cuba curves a bit at its Western end, sort of like a slightly bent finger; and just below, there's another island called the Isle of Pines. So I figured that if I hadn't spotted land at the end of two hours (the airplane did all of 80 m.p.h.), I'd turn due East, slightly to the right. That way, if I was above Cuba, I'd hit the hump of the finger; below it, I'd find the Isle of Pines.

All of which gave me an extra 5° margin of error in either direction. Some out! You'll want to know, of course, whether I ever made it safely. Yes, right on the nose.

Anyway, what I'm talking about is *having an out*.

Here's an example of how this idea can be used to avoid pit-falls in speaking:

One of my recent talks was for the Quanex company, manufacturers of steel tubing. As usual, they were going to show my Dartnell film and then have me appear from behind the screen. Following my usual plan, I was to stay outside the room and enter later through the door at the front. And, of course, I made sure in advance that this door could be opened from the hall.

But what if somebody inadvertently closed and *locked* the door? What then?

As is often the case, the tables were set in two tiers; each tier against the wall with a wide aisle down the middle. So before the meeting began, I moved the tables on one side *away* from the wall, leaving a narrow aisle along that wall.

Aha! An out!

In conformance with Murphy's Law, the sales manager, who introduced the program, stood at the front of the room throughout the film and casually locked the door from the inside!

No big problem. I used my out.

2) Don't let 'em know it. If something goes wrong, and there's no out available, the best thing to do—if you can—is to conceal it.

For instance, when a juggler drops a ball, he does a trick with it as it's bouncing up off the floor. He makes you think that this is what he *intended* to do all the time.

Same way in speaking. If you get your sequence a little out of whack, don't say, "I meant to tell you about this earlier." Who has to know? Just go on about your business and tie it in some way.

Once again, the psychology of an audience is such that they *want* you to succeed. Why let them down when you don't have to?

Marshall Granger is sales manager for a wholesale electronics firm. In running meetings, he formerly let every little goof become exposed to his sales force. Now, using the technique of *hiding* his mistakes, he's become far more forceful in the eyes of his men. So *they* perform more miracles for *him*!

Again, that's Platform Power at work.

Or, as my dad used to say, "Make your mistakes with *precision!*"

3) Make a gag out of it. If you don't have an out, and there's no way you can hide the blunder, your next best bet is to make a gag out of it.

In this connection, here's a mistake I made just last month, a few days after those seminars in Frankfurt, West Germany, and Akron, Ohio. The affair was the annual Distinguished Salesman Award banquet for the Houston Sales and Marketing Executives. I was the M.C.

Now, as I've said, I generally prefer not to use notes. So I made a point of memorizing my opening remarks, a couple of jokes that fit the occasion, my introduction of the featured speaker and so on. No problem.

But, obviously, I could *not* remember the names of all the people receiving the D.S.A. award, with their companies—a total of 34.

So, following my own advice, I printed this information in big block letters, on yellow lined paper, and then stashed these notes on the shelf of the lectern. So, when I got up to begin the proceedings, my hands were empty and I could launch into my opening patter without a care in the world—confident that my notes listing the 34 names I would later announce were resting securely below.

But, as part of the ceremony, I first had to make another presentation—the "Distinguished Citizen" Award. That's when I goofed. Because, as planned, while pulling out that special plaque, I also pulled out my notes and laid them on the lectern so that I'd be ready to breeze into the other introductions without hesitation.

Unfortunately, our "Distinguished Citizen" had a speech *he* wanted to make, and he had notes *he* wanted to use, and he laid *his* notes on top of mine and walked off to the far end of the head table—taking *my* notes along with his!

Should I have foreseen this? Sure. But I didn't. And there was no out, nor any way I could logically cover.

So I simply made a gag out of it.

"Hey, Bill!" I called out. "Let me have my notes back! How do you think I can come up with all these snappy ad-libs without my notes?"

Not very funny, I realize. But better than going to pieces over it.

I saw a marvelous example of this technique at a recent Rotary Club meeting here in Houston. The speaker was Dr. Walter L. Underwood, Minister of the St. Luke's United Methodist Church. In every respect, his speech was superb.

But the thing that really turned me on was how he handled a very tough situation—one that was not of his making.

It so happens that a young man was receiving a special award for bravery that day, and this particular ceremony—which preceded Dr. Underwood's talk—was being thoroughly covered by the press. Mikes, TV cameras and tape recorders were everywhere. But only until *that* part of the program was over!

The moment Dr. Underwood got up to speak, the TV technicians immediately stepped in *front* of him and began noisily removing their equipment—including one of the mikes affixed to the lectern! Talk about rudeness!

But Walter Underwood didn't bat an eye. He simply said: "You mean you're turning me off already?"

And then he went on: "That reminds me of one time when I was introduced at a women's club luncheon. The lady said, 'I hope the speech doesn't sound too bad. Our speaker is a little out of whack today!' "

Beautiful! Miracle Platform Power at its finest.

4) **Stay in stride.** This is not as effective as the three techniques outlined above, but it can still bail you out of a tough situation. What it means, simply, is not letting an interruption or other mishap throw you off the track.

For instance, especially following a coffee break, someone may walk back into the room after the session has begun. I'll stop mid-sentence—but only long enough to look at the guy with a big smile and say: "Welcome back, Sir! Have a seat!" Then I go back to where I left off, maybe picking it up with the previous sentence, and I'm back on track.

If there's a particularly bad moment in your talk (whether of your own making or not), that's often the time to throw in a real blockbuster—a sure-fire gag, strong visual aid or something really special.

Get the listeners' minds off the negative and on to the positive; and do it as quickly as possible.

They'll forget the bad. All you have to do is give 'em some good!

Three Great Ways to Avoid Losing Your Place

Talking about forgetting things, this is one of the greatest fears of inexperienced speakers. "Suppose I lose my place?" . . . "What if I forget what I was going to say next?"

This is an age-old problem. It needn't bother you if you know how to handle the problem. Here are three tips from the pros:

1) **The Magic-Sleep Method.** This lets your subconscious do much of the memory work. Simply do your rehearsing late in the evening just before you go to bed. All night long, your subconscious will be going at it, over and over. The next day, usually, the speech is nailed.

How does it work? Darned if I know! But it does.

2) **The Miracle Think-Ahead Technique.** Honestly, the way this works is nothing short of amazing. At my workshop at last year's National Speakers Association convention, I asked for a show of hands on this, and most of the pros agreed it works for them too. Why? Who knows? But then again, who cares?

The point here is that while you're saying one thing, you *think ahead* to what you're going to say next—or even to what you're going to say 10 or 15 minutes later!

Of course, it's best to do this during an *easy* spot in your talk—one you know you have down absolutely pat. You obviously don't want to louse up what you're saying *now*, in order to do a better job later. That could cause you to louse up both parts!

And, even then, you won't learn the Think-Ahead Technique automatically. It still takes some practice—as, of course, does everything else in the book.

But it's sure worth it. It lets you stay at least one step ahead, all the way.

3) **The Carousel.** Let's say you've followed the Magic-Sleep Method—plus, of course, all the other tips way back in Chapter 2—so you have your talk down pat. And you've used the Think-Ahead Technique during your presentation to stay on top of things throughout. Yet, somehow, you get to a certain point in your speech and you draw a complete blank. It happens!

This is when you use the Carousel. It's without doubt the best thing to do when the other two methods fail you.

It means that you *go around again*. You simply *repeat* what you've just said. Or, if you want, you can say the same thing in a slightly different way. The audience will think you've done this for emphasis!

But you haven't. You've done it to give your mind a couple of free moments—so you have *time* to regroup. Almost invariably, this gets you right back on the track. The *audience* never misses a beat!

This is why the Carousel gives you true Miracle Platform Power.

The Four Best Ways to Handle Hecklers

In all candor, this section of the book may be extraneous. In most speaking situations, audiences are generally pretty polite. (Amazingly so, it seems to me, in view of all the horrible speeches they're forced to listen to!) Usually, they even laugh politely at the terrible jokes.

But, once in a while—especially in the evening following a too-long cocktail party—a heckler will crop up in an audience.

Here are the best ways I know to handle him:

1) **Ignore him.** If he's simply made a mild comment, you might try just ignoring it.

For instance, let's say you're giving a talk about a recent trip to Hawaii, and at one point, some guy says out loud: "Oh, I've been there!"

You're probably safe in going right on without special comment. No problem.

2) **Talk to him.** In the previous example, you might prefer to respond to the man instead of ignoring him.

You could say something like this: "Oh? Did you like it?" He'll probably say: "Sure did, " or simply nod his head. Either way, you proceed from there.

Again, no problem.

3) **Kid him.** Both of the above techniques presume that the heckler is not really belligerent. Just a bit loud or boisterous. If, on the other hand, he's really starting to give you a hard time, you might heckle *him* gently—somewhat the way Johnny Carson does.

When I was President of the Houston Sales and Marketing Executives Association, I had marvelous support and cooperation from virtually everyone. But from one particular individual I received nothing but flak. This man, who happened to be from England, was constantly interrupting and hampering the proceedings.

Finally, at one general meeting, when everything was rolling along in high gear, this fellow broke in with a very rude remark.

I responded: "Gosh, I thought we won our independence from you folks 200 years ago!"

It shut him up—for *that* evening, anyway.

4) **Insult him.** This is similar to number 3, but stronger. You could call it the Don Rickles method—except that Rickles uses it on everyone! The point is that when some jerk is *really* tough to deal with, emergency procedures may be called for.

Whole books have been written, containing hundreds of put-downs. Such as:

"I never forget a face, but in your case I'll make an exception!"

"There goes the best argument in the world for tighter birth control!"

As I say, these retorts can get a little strong. So they should *not* be used indiscriminately. Only when the heckler is getting really rough on *you*. And that happens very rarely.

In any case, probably the most important thing to remember in *any* difficult situation is: *KEEP YOUR COOL.*

Once again, this has to do directly with the psychology of an audience.

You see, as I've said before, the audience *wants* you to succeed. Hence, when someone begins to interfere with your presentation, *the audience doesn't like it.* Why? Because he's interfering with "*their*" presentation! *The audience likes you better than the heckler!* Their sympathies are with *you*, not him.

But, obviously, that's true only as long as you're more likeable than he is! The moment you start to lose your cool, the audience's sentiments immediately turn to the heckler.

This is one problem you *never* have to face—unless you cause it yourself.

So don't let it happen.

Keep your cool.

What to Do About Whispering

Whisperers are akin to hecklers. They annoy you—and the audience—in much the same way. They only do it more privately. But they can be just as much of a problem. And, as with the heckler, pleading to them rarely has any effect.

One way to handle the whisperer is simply to stop for a moment and look at the person. If he only has a mild case of whisperitis, that will usually quiet him down.

Or, if necessary, you can ask him in a polite tone: "Excuse me, but I didn't quite hear what you were saying." That generally works.

If two people persist in whispering loudly to each other, you can remark: "Say, can you people hear me okay? I can sure hear *you!*"

But perhaps the best way to handle a whisperer is to *just be quiet*. Dead silence! This way, the only sound in the room will be the "psst-psst" of the whispering! If this doesn't shut 'em up, probably nothing will.

Again, these methods will give you far greater Platform Power—but only when you keep your cool.

When to Leave Well Enough Alone

There's just one more thing that needs to be said about all of this.

In Chapter 4 I pointed out that the responsibility for a Platform Power environment is yours. And throughout the book I've emphasized the importance of perfection.

But, without contradicting anything I've said before, let me now make a point that it's taken me many, many years to learn:

It's possible to be *too* much of a perfectionist. Sometimes it's best to leave well enough alone.

Just a few years ago, in Atlanta, I was on a program with a number of my friends on the circuit—many of whose names are mentioned throughout this book.

As customary, my live presentation was preceded by a showing of my film. Except that, in this instance, because of the unusually strict time limitations, it was possible to show only a *very brief clip* of the film—about two minutes.

I checked everything out meticulously; loaded the film into the projector so the clip would begin on precisely the right frame; made sure it was perfectly zeroed in on the screen; the sound and focus were right; and so on.

So, when the film began, everything was in order and all was right with the world.

But then I noticed that the sound was just a *hair* too low. And, as a perfectionist, I rushed over to turn it louder, which was a *bad* mistake!

When I fiddled with the darn thing, the projector lamp blew, the screen went black, there wasn't time to fix it or start over, and half of that brief movie clip was missed.

In line with the suggestion I offered earlier in this chapter, I did make a gag out of it as best I could, saying: "I've heard of X-rated movies, but this is ridiculous!" And my talk went fine.

But not as fine as it would have if I had let well enough alone.

So, when the mike is okay, *leave it alone*. When the temperature is about right, *leave it alone*. When your props are in place, *leave 'em alone*.

Especially *during* the presentation itself. Otherwise, once more, Murphy's Law will do you in. Quit while you're ahead.

MIRACLE PLATFORM POWER CAPSULE

1) Anything that <u>can</u> go wrong, <u>will</u> go wrong:
   It's up to you to prevent it.

2) The key is preparation:
   You have to get there early.

3) Complex presentations require extra preparation:
   The early bird gets the applause.

4) Know what to do when something <u>does</u> go wrong:
   Make your mistakes with precision.

5) Remember how to avoid losing your place:
   The Magic-Sleep Method; The Think-Ahead; The Carousel.

6) Don't let hecklers hog the spotlight:
   Ignore 'em; Talk to 'em; Kid 'em; Insult 'em.

7) Whisperers, like hecklers, need to be quieted:
   They annoy both you and the audience.

8) It's possible to be too much of a perfectionist:
   Know when to quit while you're ahead.

9

Building Platform Power Rapport With Your Audience

Which Is More Important: You or Your Speech?

This is without doubt *the* most important chapter in the book.

For, while we've been talking about the psychology of an audience—and how to get it working in your favor—ever since we started out, at this point we're going to concentrate on this *one* critical aspect to better public speaking. Without it, you'll never get past mediocrity. With it, you're a star.

The first step to acquiring that mystical ingredient of "stage presence"—the first thing you *must* do for real "platform charisma"—is to recognize this all-important fact:

YOU ARE MORE IMPORTANT THAN YOUR SPEECH!

I first recognized this when I was a night club magician, over 30 years ago.

People never applauded (or hissed) the tricks I performed; they applauded (or hissed) *me*. As I found out then, if the audience liked *me*, the magic itself didn't really matter. If they *didn't* like me, the greatest miracle in the world wouldn't bail me out.

Johnny Carson obviously discovered the same truth. When *he* became a star, he dropped the magic act that he'd started out with; just as W.C. Fields eliminated his juggling and Jack Benny packed away his violin. Even Bing Crosby—he won an Academy Award for his *acting* ability, not his singing.

So what you *are* is more important than what you *say*.

In fact, talking about singing, look at all the truly fine vocalists we've enjoyed over the past generations—Tony Bennett, Jerry Vale, and Dick Haymes, to mention just a few. All these men—and others like them—have had splendid voices. They all became stars.

But, they did *not* achieve the fame—nor the financial rewards—of Bing Crosby, Frank Sinatra, or Dean Martin, for example. Why? Because of the difference in their approach to *audience psychology*.

Call it sex appeal, or whatever. The point is that we pay greatest homage to those entertainers whom we *like* as human beings.

It's the same way in public speaking. Audiences rarely give standing ovations to speeches. They applaud the *speaker*.

How to Develop a Winning Style

There's an old saying in this business that if you steal something from one man, it's robbery; if you steal from a thousand, it's *research!*

So, all of us on the speaking circuit do a certain amount of "research" from time to time. We all learn from each other.

And that's as it should be. After all, virtually every worthwhile idea known to man was enunciated at one time or another by Ben

Franklin or William Shakespeare—and, prior to that, by the Bible. There's nothing *totally* new under the sun.

So, by all means, it's wise to study and learn from other speakers. Especially now, with cassette tapes so readily and inexpensively available, it's ridiculous *not* to benefit from the experience of others. That, I realize, is precisely why you're reading this book!

But—and this is the point I've been leading up to—*emulate but don't imitate.*

According to Webster, "emulate" means "to strive to equal or excel." It does *not* mean to *copy*. There is a difference.

All of which means, of course, that you have to develop *your own* winning style.

Dr. Charles Jarvis once said to me: "John, you'll always be in demand, because you're *different*. The guys who want to be another Bill Gove simply don't realize that if they succeed in that effort, people won't hire *them*—they'll hire Bill Gove!" Amen.

I mention Charles Jarvis here because he is without a doubt one of the very finest examples of what I'm talking about. He is a very, very funny guy, but there's no way in the world for you (or me) to make *his* material as funny as *he* does.

For instance, this bit. I'll give it to you exactly as he gave it to me for inclusion in the book (bear in mind that Charles used to be a dentist). Here it is:

"Woman came in one day. Had a dog with her. Yeah. Big dog—a Doberman. Walking in front of her, carrying a blanket in his mouth. No, I did not tell the dog to get out, Turkey. You don't tell a Doberman to get out. You might tell a poodle to get out, but you don't tell no Doberman to get out. You do and you'll regret it, that's the gospel truth.

"I was a Fuller Brush man when I went to Dental School there in Houston. Yeah, had the Eastern district. Lots of dogs. Little dogs, big dogs, fast dogs, slow dogs. You get to know 'em. Not only did I get to know 'em. I got to where I looked for the signs in the yards: 'Beware of the dog.' Yeah. I believed 'em, too. If a sign was real little, I still saw it—'cause I was looking for it.

"Even those little, bitty dogs—terriers—they are a bother to

you. You, going along with your bag full of brushes and that mop
and broom over your shoulder, and this little terrier, yelping and
nipping at your Achilles tendon. You're sure at any minute he's
gonna nip into it, but you go along, sweating, and trying not to act
like you're scared he's gonna nip into it.

"But a Doberman—now that, friend, is a different matter.
Doberman, he won't go for the Achilles tendon. Right for the
groin. Yeah. Leave the ground ten feet away from you and attach
to your groin. Yeah. Boy, that smarts! A Doberman hanging on
your groin. Ain't a good feeling at all.

"So I didn't tell him to get out. No way. I didn't like him coming into my operatory. You know, we try to keep those areas clean,
sterile and all that. You don't want dog hairs everywhere. Patients
kinda picky about that sort of thing. Dog hairs—or any kind of
hairs.

"Friend of mine quit a dentist once on account of hair, or
hairs, or something hairy. She never really knew *what* it was. Just
said everytime she went in to see that dentist, and looked under his
laboratory door, there it was—whatever it was. Fuzzy, she said.
Funny looking, yet menacing looking. Scared her. Scared her
plumb away from that dentist. Said she was always afraid whatever
it was was gonna run out of there at her. Probably was just broom
fuzz, stuff he had swept up years ago. Wouldn't have run at her.
Kinda picky, I thought.

"Anyway, this dog came in with this woman. Had this blanket
in his mouth, rolled up. He walked right into operatory #1 like he
had been there before, went over into the corner behind the dental
unit, dropped the blanket, rolled it out with his nose, and lay down
there on the blanket. Every now and then he would growl, kinda
fierce like—low growl, like he didn't like the room or something.

"The lady sat down. I looked in her mouth, trying not to
notice the dog there in the corner. But when he would growl, it
bothered me a bit. She would raise up a little in the chair, lean up,
and shout coarsely, 'Shut up over there! You hear me? Shut up!'

"I whispered to her 'Don't rile him.' (I could just see that dog
in mid-air. Right for my groin!)

"I ventured, 'That dog looks like he could be real mean.'

"She shot back, 'He is mean—and he don't like to see me hurt, either.'

"I took the hint. That lady had it easy that day."

You'll find other Jarvis humor in the "Ready-Reference Story Teller's Guide" at the back of the book. But you won't find this one.

You won't find it because it's uniquely *his*. If you've ever heard him speak, you can just *see* him delivering it. You can't see *yourself* (or anyone else) doing it. When Charles does it, it's an absolute riot. But *only* when *he* does it.

Every other prominent speaker mentioned in this book has *his* own style.

So you must have *yours*.

Style Comes from Within

You'll note that Charles Jarvis calls upon his experiences as a dentist.

Jim Gillie scores with stories about his Arkansas background, delivered in a dry Will Rogers-ish manner.

Cavett Robert relates back to his experiences growing up in Mississippi.

Roy Hatten capitalizes on his skill as a magician.

In my own case, I get a lot of mileage out of my boyhood in Hawaii, and my exploits as a private pilot.

In the same way, *you* have experiences that are uniquely *yours*, and your *own* background is your best source for a winning style.

Or, to put it another way, the best way to develop your own style is to *make sure it's no one else's!* And, conversely, that way no one else's style can copy *yours!*

Now, obviously, I've referred here to many of my fellow pros on the circuit—partly because they *are* pros and epitomize what we're talking about, besides which, of course, I'm familiar with their work.

But, this business of developing a winning style is *not* restricted to speaking professionally. Not by any means. No matter where you speak, how often or for whom, *you* can follow the same principles.

As a "non-pro" example, take Mike Schuler, impressive, young head basketball coach at Rice University in Houston. Since Mike is, by profession, a coach, he is clearly *not* a "professional" speaker.

But, he sure acts like one on the platform! And it's largely because of his own unique *style*—taken from his own experiences.

For instance, in talking about the occasional difficulty of getting through to his players, Mike relates the time he tried to sell the team on the evils of liquor.

To illustrate the point, Mike (according to the story) held out two drinking glasses—one filled with water, the other with gin. He dropped a worm into the glass of water; it swam merrily about. He then placed the worm in the gin; it immediately curled up and died.

"Okay," Mike then said to his players, "what lesson does this teach us?"

"That's easy, Coach," one seven-footer answered. "If you drink enough gin you won't have worms!"

Again, this is *style*, which leads to Miracle Platform Power.

Your Platform Power Style Check-List

Okay, we're agreed that to develop Miracle Platform Power, you need your own unique speaking *style*. And, further, that this style should, ideally, come from your own personal experience.

On the next page, you will find a Platform Power Style Check-List—calculated to help you achieve this all-important goal in public speaking.

Here, now, is how you can use the Check-List to develop your own unique speaking style:

1) **Your Age.** Fill in the answer. Then write down how you can *use* this in your speaking.

For instance, as already mentioned, the great Red Motley says: "I'm delighted to be here. Hell, at my age, I'm delighted to be anywhere!" *Style!*

PLATFORM POWER STYLE CHECK-LIST

Considerations	Answers	How to Use in Speaking
Your Age		
Place of Birth or Childhood		
Family		
Physical Characteristics		
Profession		
Hobbies		
Favorite Comedian		

**Let Your Own Experiences Develop Your Own Style
...Then It Can't Be Anyone Else's**

Lawrence Wayne, bright young Harris County judge, being only 35 (and looking younger), remarks: "Yes, I know I'm young for a judge, but I'll get over it!" *Style!*

2) Place of Birth or Childhood. See how you can capitalize on it to develop your own speaking style.

Numerous examples have already been cited.

3) Family. Here again, this offers many clues.

Henny Youngman is world-famous for his, "Take my wife—please!"

Herb True, one of the real platform pros, talks about his eight children. "Anyone with eight kids," says Herb, "is either a Catholic or a Protestant who isn't paying attention!" *Style!*

4) Physical Characteristics. Jimmy Durante and Danny Thomas have capitalized on their oversized noses.

Robert Henry, a rising star on the banquet circuit, makes his huge bulk a personal trademark.

5) Profession. Again, I've already given you many examples.

6) Hobbies. Bob Hope often uses a golf club as a prop. And where would Groucho Marx have been without his cigar?

7) Favorite Comedian. What is *your* style?

Personally, I feel most comfortable emulating (not imitating!) the casual manner of Johnny Carson or Jack Benny. You may prefer the raconteur-style of Myron Cohen, or the machine-gun delivery of Bob Hope. The decision is *yours.*

Again, you'll never achieve real Platform Power by simply copying someone else.

The style has to be *your own.*

And the Platform Power Style Check-List will help you develop it.

Confidence vs. Arrogance

As I've pointed out repeatedly, you want to put your audience totally at ease—and, to do that, *you* have to appear totally at ease.

Note that I said "appear" totally at ease—which is not at all to say that you should be completely *relaxed*. Far from it. For when you're 100% relaxed, you're asleep! And it's tough to make a coherent speech in that condition!

So, if you have a few butterflies in your stomach, fine! That just means that your nervous energy is at work and the adrenalin is flowing—all of which is necessary for you to be in top form.

Or, as one speech trainer put it: "Don't ever expect to *eliminate* the butterflies—just get 'em to fly in formation!"

So, as I was saying, you have to project an air of confidence. But now, here's the point I was leading up to:

Confidence does not mean arrogance. There's a huge difference between the two.

Once again, your primary job is to get people to like you. And they *will* like you if you come across as a confident, congenial, convivial sort of guy or gal.

They *won't* like you if you seem to be an arrogant S.O.B.

So, try to avoid talking down to your audience.

Use phrases like: "As you know . . .", "I know you've heard some of this before, but . . .", "Here are some ideas I'd like to share with you," and so forth.

Same way, it's a good idea to quote other people.

Sure, it's fine to relate back to your own experiences, as I suggested in the previous section. But not *all* the time. If you weave in the statements of others, too, that lends additional credence to everything *you* say—and makes you more *likeable* at the same time.

Even Don Rickles tempers his insults with occasional humility!

How to Turn Faces into Friends

By definition, public speaking is speaking in *public*—talking to a *crowd*.

And, as I pointed out in Chapter 4, it's best to crowd your listeners *together* so they're not spread too far apart.

But still, *you cannot make friends with a sea of faces*. You can only make friends with *people*.

Which, as I've been saying all along, is what Platform Power is all about—making *friends* with your listeners.

How can you do this? The same way you make friends at a cocktail party or on the job: *You develop direct personal contact*.

Now, obviously, you cannot do this with 50 or 5000 people individually. But the beautiful thing about it is: *You don't have to*.

The fact is—and, once again, this is part of the psychology of an audience—when you develop direct contact with a *few* people in your audience, you make friends with *all!* That's the way it works.

When Rich Little is introduced at the Riviera Hotel in Las Vegas, the first thing he does is *shake hands* with someone at a ringside table. The reaction of the audience is: "Hey, he's got a friend! *I'll* be his friend, too!" That's Miracle Platform Power at work.

A similar technique, used by many speakers, is to address certain members of the audience by name. After making a statement, for instance, you can say to someone (when it pertains): "You've seen that happen, haven't you, Charlie?" The rest of your listeners somehow feel that you've spoken to *them* individually, too!

Once, following a seminar for the Utah Realtors Association at Lake Tahoe, my wife and I attended a Joey Bishop show at Harrah's Hotel. My wife, Alice, happens to be an extremely attractive gal—besides which I properly greased the palm of the maitre d'—so, for both of those reasons, we got the best table in the house, front row center, right against the stage.

All during the show, I became Joey Bishop's foil, and we kidded back and forth during the entire hour he was on. Did this add to my enjoyment of the evening? You betcha. But it also added to the enjoyment of the *other* folks, too.

In my own seminars, I often pick a cheerful-looking guy in the front and use certain remarks to him as a sort of running gag throughout the program.

When I introduce my "Legend of Cautious Cassius"—which

is a story about using time more efficiently—I'll look directly at my foil in the front and say, kiddingly, "You didn't know I wrote a legend, did you?"

Later, when I recite my poem, "The Salesman" (which you'll see in the next chapter), I look back at the same guy and say: "You didn't know I wrote a poem, did you?"

Again, this makes friends with the *entire* audience—and it's also part of my *style*.

Similarly, even in a short 30-minute address, one of my favorite stunts is to auction off a unique mousetrap contraption to prove, "If you build a better mousetrap, people will *not* beat a path to your door." You still have to *sell* it to get top dollar. (I've gotten as much as $10 for the silly thing. But, again, I want the audience to *like* me, so I always tell the top bidder to give the $10—or whatever—to charity, and he still keeps the mousetrap.)

Anyway, my point here in the book is this: While only a handful of people participate in the stunt directly—those who actually enter the bidding—the *entire audience* feels involved!

And in longer seminars, I get certain people onto the stage to compete actively in role-playing exercises. Here, the entire audience votes on the winner.

I once did a seminar in Honolulu, for the Foodland International Corporation of Atlanta. Following the role-playing bit, as the six contestants lined up with their backs to the audience, ready for the vote, one of the men said: "I wonder what he's going to have us do now—bend over?"

Again, this got a big laugh from the entire audience—and it's a line I've repeated ever since!

So those are just a few examples as to how you can make *friends* with your audience for greater Platform Power.

Just two words of warning:

First, *avoid "inside" jokes*. Occasionally, you'll see a nightclub comedian kidding with the band about something the audience knows nothing about. This is bad business! If there's a joke somewhere, let the audience in on it.

Second, *don't embarrass people*. Talk to them, kid them, play with them—that's fine. But don't make fools of them. If you do, you'll create enemies instead of friends.

Following the first of four annual meetings that I conducted for the American Express Company, their Vice President, George Waters, commented: "Nobody objected to your horseplay, because you *complimented* all who participated. Everyone came out a *winner*."

Once again, your job as a speaker is to make friends.

Five Steps to Greater Vocal Command

As a speaker, you do a great many things on the platform to win over your audience. That's why this book has 11 chapters.

But, obviously, your main job as a speaker is to *speak*. You and I are *talking* animals.

Hence, the proper use of your *voice* is of primary importance.

A good part of all this, of course, is like your physiognomy. It's something you were born with, and you can't totally change it.

Among the pros on the circuit, for instance, Ty Boyd and Carl Winters are two men to whom God gave marvelously pleasing voices. If He was equally kind to you, you're indeed fortunate.

But, just as you can better your appearance through proper grooming, you can improve your voice through the application of proven techniques—and, again, through *practice*.

Here are some good rules to remember:

1) **Say what you mean.** One of the great qualities of the English language is its exactness. Whatever idea you want to convey, there's usually a word that describes it precisely. Use the right word.

2) **Widen your vocabulary.** The only way to follow Rule #1 is to have *enough* words at your command. Not necessarily big words. Short words, in simple sentences, are often better. But avoid limiting your speech to too *few*—especially the overworked words like "cool" and "super" and "you know." Spice your speech with variety!

3) **Pronounce with precision.** When you decide on a word to say, *say* it. Speak distinctly; stay away from slurs. Say: "Did you?"—not "Didja?" . . . "I've got to"—not "I gotta." Pay "attention" to your pronunciation—not "tenshun!"

4) **Vary the notes.** An important way to interest listeners is to *pitch* your voice at different levels. You tend to bore people when you talk in a monotone. Your voice covers a wide range of notes—so ride the range!

5) **Be a stop-and-go talker.** It's helpful to vary your vocal *speed*, too. People get confused—or go to sleep—listening to a steady drone. Pauses win you attention—and emphasize the points you want to get across. In any case, *don't talk too slowly.*

Of course, a good P.A. system helps immeasurably. You can literally whisper into a mike and be plainly heard throughout an auditorium.

And, talking about P.A. systems, all of these techniques can—and should—be practiced with a tape recorder.

Similarly, it's an excellent idea to carry a cassette recorder with you and lay it on the lectern during your speech. That way, you'll hear how you actually sound "live" on the platform.

And then you can practice further improvement.

Dave Yoho was born with a distinct speech impediment. Overcoming this through years of practice, he has become one of the very finest (and most successful) speakers on the professional circuit.

My own public speaking prof at Dartmouth told me that I didn't have a very good, naturally resonant voice. He was right. I didn't. I still don't.

I guess I've learned to *use* it.

The Magic Ingredient

Here, to close this chapter, is probably the simplest—yet most often ignored—secret to greater Platform Power.

A smile. That's it: *a smile.*

Again, think of headline entertainers. Bob Hope's sly grin has become almost a trademark. So has Dean Martin's devilish leer. And Johnny Carson's smile is absolutely infectious.

Jane Pauley, of NBC's Today Show, is a most attractive and charming young lady. Notice how that charm is enhanced by her delightful smile.

Among professional speakers, Charles Jarvis' pixie-ish face totally lights up—and practically lights up the whole room.

In my own case, candidly, I've learned that I *have* to smile. There was a slight war in the 1940's—which you may or may not remember—and I happen to have a scar on my left cheek. Watching myself on TV, I found out years ago that when I *don't* smile, I look as if I'm frowning!

So I make a point of *smiling* when I speak.

And this, too, like everything else, can be *practiced*.

Try standing in front of a mirror. Go through various facial exercises, to discover which smile appears most appealing.

Further, you can have a photographer take a series of shots of you using strobe lights. See which ones you—and others around you—like the best.

Then *use* that smile during every speech.

Obviously, you don't want to look silly, and there are (or certainly should be) places in your talk where any smile would admittedly be out of place.

Nor do you ever want your smile to seem insincere. That becomes a real turn-off.

But an honest, genuine smile can boost your Miracle Platform Power tremendously.

Smile and the audience smiles with you.

MIRACLE PLATFORM POWER CAPSULE

1) You are more important than your speech:
   When they like <u>you</u>, they'll like what <u>you</u> say.
2) Don't try to copy someone else's style:
   A winning style has to be your own.

3) Style comes from within:
   Use your own experiences; then they can't be anyone else's.

4) Complete the Platform Power Style Check-List:
   Then, all you have to do is <u>use</u> it.

5) Be confident, but not arrogant:
   There's a world of difference between the two.

6) Make friends with individuals:
   That way, you make friends with the crowd.

7) Follow the 5 steps to greater vocal command:
   A better talker is a better speaker.

8) Remember the magic ingredient:
   Nothing is more likeable than a smile.

10

How Platform Power Guarantees Your Applause

The Grand Finale

If there's one part of your talk that's more important than the beginning, it's the end. This is the last—and hopefully the lasting—impression you leave with your audience.

And also, of course, the end is when they applaud. With a mediocre finale, you'll always get at least a polite smattering of hand-clapping. But, throw in a strong, compelling close and they'll really get up and cheer!

So make sure your final hook is a blockbuster. Something they'll applaud now and remember later.

Again, as I've emphasized repeatedly throughout the book, all of this has to be meticulously *planned* and *rehearsed*. The very worst thing you can do is let your talk simply trail off into nothingness. (We've all heard speakers who didn't even seem to know when they were finished!)

This chapter will give you some proven, audience-tested closes you can use for more Platform Power every time you speak.

Planning for a Stronger Ending

According to some of the pros on the circuit, the best way to close is with a gag. I've already referred (in Chapter 6) to George M. Cohan's line: "Always leave 'em laughing." That philosophy clearly worked for him.

But, again as I've repeated throughout, audiences rarely applaud a speech. They applaud the *speaker*. And this is why you'll almost invariably get a better response when you leave 'em thinking and doing—all of which comes when they remember *you* more than your speech. (As I also pointed out in Chapter 6, even big-name comedians like Bob Hope and Red Skelton often end on a serious note: an appeal to some charity, for instance.)

So your first decision in this whole regard is to determine what there is about your subject matter—and, even more importantly, what there is about *you*—that you want your listeners to remember.

In giving a speech on estate planning, for example, here are some of the possible impressions you may want to leave with your audience:

1) The tragedy of a destitute widow;
2) The joy of an affluent retirement;
3) Your own expertise on the subject; or
4) Your concern for the welfare of your listeners.

These are all strong points. You might come out fine closing on any of them. But if *I* were doing it, I'd close on the *last* one.

Why? Simply because that's what I'd want the audience to remember about *me*.

So I'd figure out some way to get this point across strongly, and I'd end on that note.

Does this sound cold and calculating? Sure it does! But that's what the whole book is all about—achieving Miracle Platform Power on *purpose*, not by accident.

How to Close with a Bang

Of course, the easiest way to close your speech effectively is simply to summarize your main points briefly, and then call for action—which, again, is (or should be) your whole objective in speaking.

Like a salesman, your job is to "get the order."

But, as I suggested in the previous section, it's best to tie it all together with a final, rousing example. In speaking about fire prevention, for instance, you could end with a story about a child who dragged his sleeping parents from their burning home; you might close a political speech by quoting the words on the Statue of Liberty; Etc., etc.

Or, if you have some startling bit of showmanship that is calculated to bring cheers from your audience, be sure to use *that* for your grand finale. (Notice how top-flight magicians always save their biggest stunt for last.)

Rolland Storey, for instance, closes with a special recorded song about Americanism. It's admittedly sheer (though totally sincere) flag-waving. But that's what Rolland's speech is all about. This close usually gets a standing ovation.

In the same way, Dave Yoho often ends with an inspirational plea for excellence, which is spoken over recorded music. It's powerful stuff!

In any case, the close must *climax* your entire presentation. It should be the most powerful weapon in your arsenal—a blast that stirs your listeners' *emotions* as well as their minds.

As you've gathered, my own talks are usually to sales and business groups. So I often close with a poem I wrote several years ago, titled "The Salesman," which follows on the next page.

You're welcome to use it if you want. Please, just give me credit!

I can tell you that I've used this close in talks and seminars on four continents, and I find it's almost like playing "Anchors Aweigh" at an Annapolis reunion!

How and When to Say "Thank You" for Greater Applause

Have you ever noticed all the "applause-builders" that are used in a Las Vegas night club? The curtains, the lights, the movements of the performer—all are orchestrated to achieve the desired effect.

And applause is contagious. The more some people clap, the more others clap. When some people stand, others stand. Which is obviously what you want to happen.

As speakers, you and I rarely have Las Vegas lighting and stage technicians working for us. But we can use at least *some* of the same techniques.

And the essential rule is: Let the audience *know* when the end is coming and the applause is expected.

Do *not* say, "And in closing" a dozen times before you get to the close. That just lets the audience know you're not really prepared—and also scares 'em into thinking you're going to be rambling on forever!

But do tell 'em once—immediately prior to your big finish— that the end is coming. Use *that* moment to thank them for their warm hospitality, etc. Here, you have plenty of *time* for these remarks.

Then, when you deliver your "socko" close, you don't have to keep talking after you've finished. The second you're ready to sit down, the audience is ready to cheer!

The end is the end.

THE SALESMAN
by John Wolfe

When labor toils and factories hum
And out plant doors the products come,
The payment for it all comes from
    The Salesman.

In any business office, where
White collar workers earn their share,
They all should thank in grateful prayer
    The Salesman.

When banks and institutions lend
The funds on which the firms depend
For finance, they, too, have a friend—
    The Salesman.

And miles of gleaming railroad track
And roads and highways there and back
Could not exist without his knack—
    The Salesman.

So 'cross the land, behind each door,
Are worlds of wealth and goods galore.
They'd ne'er be there—were it not for
    The Salesman.

Yes, others may salute their trade,
The contributions they have made;
But it's for him that I'll parade—
    The Salesman.

For it is sales that keep us free,
That fuel our great democracy,
And that is why I'm proud to be
    A Salesman.

The Most Powerful Close in the World

I'm devoting this entire section to a close which I've used repeatedly over the years. I call it "the most powerful close in the world" because that, in my opinion, is precisely what it is.

I hasten to say that it isn't my invention. I first heard it told by Kip Anger, the inspiring marketing V.P. at Zenith Television. Bob Richards, former Olympic star and Wheaties champion, has used it many times. So has Roy Hatten. So, I'm sure, have others.

Too bad! I wish it were all mine! But it isn't

And, in fact, a song about it was recorded not too long ago.

So, invariably, some people in any audience will have heard it. More, I guess, after this book gets read. No matter. I'll still use it. So can you, with almost any audience. Here is how I tell it:

I'm going to close now with a story—a *true* story. We've had a lot of laughs here today, and it's really been great being with you folks—honest, I've enjoyed it tremendously and I really appreciate your hospitality.

But this isn't a joke. It's all true. Maybe some of you have heard it before—it's been told many times—and when I even think about it, I crack a little. But I think it carries a message—about that little extra effort that's needed to make all these things work.

It's a football story, and it was told originally by Lou Little, the great coach at Columbia University, who was sort of a Vince Lombardi of his day. And it all happened, it's all in the record books.

One day this green, green freshman ran out on the field. Freshmen could play varsity football then—as they can now, but couldn't for many years. And this fellow had such marvelous spirit and enthusiasm, it was beautiful!

The only trouble was: He couldn't play football! Couldn't run, block, tackle, kick, pass—nothing! So Lou Little said to the kid: "Look, you're a great guy; but we've got no place for you on this team."

Well, apparently, the other guys on the team thought so much of this kid—they just liked him so well—they went to Lou Little, in a group, and said: "Coach, we know this guy can't play worth a darn, but we'd like to have him with us on the team. So why don't you give him a uniform, give him a number and keep him on the sidelines. He doesn't have to play—we'd just like to have him with us on the team."

So that's what they did. And every Saturday, as the team ran out under that golden arch, here was this kid in uniform, with the rest of the team. Even though he never played a single minute, in a single game, all during his freshman, sophomore, junior, and senior year.

Until. The last game of his senior year was against Army—Columbia meeting mighty Army!—which was something in itself.

And it just so happens that Monday of that week—the week of the big game—this kid's father suddenly died.

So Lou Little went over to the kid—they were close by then—and he said: "Look, I don't know how to tell you how we all feel about this, our sympathy, but why don't you go home, take care of the family." (Apparently, he was the oldest son.)

"And, obviously, don't worry about football, but don't worry about your studies, either—somehow, we'll help you make them up. Go home, do what you have to do, come back whenever you feel like it."

And Friday of that week, this kid buried his father.

And the next day, Saturday, as the team ran out under that golden arch to meet mighty Army, here was this kid in uniform with the rest of the team!

Lou Little went over to him and said: "Hey, what are you doing here? I thought you'd be home."

The kid said: "I haven't bothered you—for four years, I've never bugged you once—but today I want to play in that game!"

Well, as you can imagine, Lou Little had this tremendous responsibility to the team, the school, the trustees, the alumni—but he hated to say no to the kid. So he thought, "Well, maybe I'll let him in for the opening kick-off. If Army receives, someone will tackle the guy; if Columbia receives, the kid will be up front, out of the way. Can't do any harm."

So that's what they did. As I said, this is all true, it's all in the record books.

As it turned out, Army won the toss and elected to receive. Columbia kicked off. The Army man who caught the ball was stopped, dead in his tracks, on the three-yard line—by, you guessed it, this kid.

Lou Little thought, "It's a fluke, it's a miracle, it won't happen again for a million years—but I can't take him out now. Maybe I'll leave him in for one more play"

On the opening play from scrimmage, the Army quarterback was tackled behind the goal line, in the end zone, for a 2-point safety—by, you guessed it, this kid.

It turned out that *those were the only two points scored by either team all afternoon.*

The kid was in every play . . . he was the undisputed hero of the day . . . they carried him off on their shoulders . . . the locker room was a madhouse.

Finally, it thinned out a little, and Lou Little went over to the kid, sat down next to him and put his arm around his shoulder, and said: "That's got to be the most magnificent thing I've ever seen on a football field. But, for God's sake, tell me: For four years you've been sitting on the sidelines. Why didn't you ever show me you could play football like that?"

The kid said: "Coach, I don't think I ever *could* play football like that. But, you see, I never told you: My father was blind—but I figured, *today he's going to watch me play football.*"

And that's what we're really talking about: the extra effort and dedication that makes all the difference—in business, in our personal lives, in this whole silly world.

Ladies and Gentlemen, you've been just wonderful, and if anything we've said today helps *you* use your extra effort and dedication more effectively, I'll be most grateful—and, surely, you are all Aces.

MIRACLE PLATFORM POWER CAPSULE

1) Let your finale be a <u>grand</u> finale:
   It's your last—and <u>lasting</u>—impression.

2) Let 'em remember <u>you</u> even more than your speech:
   That's the way to <u>plan</u> it.
3) Close with an appeal to <u>emotions!</u>
   That's how to "get the order."
4) Let the audience know when the end is coming:
   Then stop when you're finished.
5) Use the most powerful close in the world:
   There's nothing stronger.

11

How to Continue Building Your Miracle Platform Power

The Never-Ending Process of Improvement

I started Chapter 1 by suggesting that professionalism in public speaking is largely a matter of *attitude*—of doing the very best job possible.

I'll begin this last chapter by saying that this same professional attitude also demands constant striving for *further* improvement. Or, to put it another way, the pro is never satisfied with his own current performance.

This, of course, is why N.F.L. football stars continue their daily drills, P.G.A. golfers still take lessons, and top musicians never stop practicing. They all know that when you stop getting better, you stop being good.

The same, obviously, applies to public speaking.

So, if you haven't done so before, right now might be a good time to set down some specific goals for yourself. Think about it for a few minutes. What, in particular, is there about *your* Platform Power that you most want to improve? To what degree? When? *Write down your answers—in specific terms.*

Then, as you build your Miracle Platform Power over the coming months and years, you can measure your progess against these goals.

In his excellent book, *Forging Ahead in Magic*, John Booth comments that great magicians rarely indulge in idle practice. They rehearse their tricks with *specific* objectives in mind—to conceal each bit of sleight-of-hand in a certain way, etc.

You can follow the same rule in improving your speaking ability. Perfect *one* aspect of your Platform Power. . . then another . . . then another . . . until you have it *all* down pat.

And then work some more, because improvement is a never-ending process.

In his highly entertaining and inspirational message "The Abominable Snowjob," Charles Jarvis points out the fact that too many of us—in all fields of endeavor—seem to be satisfied with our own status quo. And, further, that we tend to blame others for our own shortcomings.

As Charlie points out, this has been going on a very long time. When the Lord accused Adam of misbehavior in the Garden of Eden, Adam said, in effect: "It's all Eve's fault. *She* made me do it!" And when the Lord turned his wrath on Eve, she said, in effect: "Don't look at me! The *serpent* is to blame!"

We all fall into this trap at times. If nothing else, we claim that whatever we do—or don't do—is "just the way we are."

I call this "I'm Me-ism"—and, in fact, I wrote another poem about this insidious disease. It goes like this:

Here I am in all my glory;
Here I am for all to see.
I gotta say that I ain't much;
    That's O.K.—I'm me.

I always hear of better things
That I could do or be.
Never get around to doing them;
    That's O.K.—I'm me.

Big things that could change my life,
Bring real prosperity;
I always seem to leave 'em lying there;
    That's O.K.—I'm me.

Little things that mean so much
To home and family:
I don't pay 'em no attention;
    That's O.K.—I'm me.

Oh, there's got to be a better way
To peace and harmony.
How to find it? I ain't lookin'!
    That's O.K.—I'm me.

Yes, gifts in life are for the giver;
That's in history.
Me? I'm just too busy taking!
    That's O.K.—I'm me.

So when I come to meet my Maker,
I'll say to Him, you'll see:
"I know I'm goin' straight to Hell!
    But that's O.K.—I'm me!"

My point, of course, is that it's *not* O.K. to just "be yourself"—unless you're the *best* "yourself" possible.

The great Herb True, whom I've mentioned before, is one of the real pros on the circuit. He gives hundreds of top-notch speeches every year. But he still records practically every talk, and then listens to it later with his associates—all in order to raise his level of perfection still further.

That's one reason Herb is a pro.

How to Learn from the Experts

You've noticed that throughout this book, I've made continual references to *professional* speakers—and also to performers in many fields of show business.

I realize that, in your own case, you may never aspire to earning a living on the platform, but as I've said, Miracle Platform Power works in *any* speaking environment. It's an ability that will profit you greatly regardless of your line of work. And it's certainly a great avocation.

But, you can still learn from the experts.

This is why it's important to attend professional seminars, concert appearances and night club shows. Watch what top performers do and how they do it—relative to all the points made throughout this book. See how *they* use audience psychology, exactly as I've indicated.

And finally, as I've suggested previously, if you're serious about effective speaking, you should by all means join the National Speakers Association, headquartered in Phoenix, Arizona. As of this writing, its membership numbers about 800—and will surely be considerably higher by the time you read this book.

Among other activities, N.S.A. holds an annual convention—usually in the summer—which is an absolute *treasure* of solid platform know-how, furnished by the best in the business. And, at the same time, it's a thrilling experience. (Even the invocations deserve standing ovations!)

One final point in this connection.

While you can, as I say, learn best from experts, you can also learn from all the duffers that you hear most of the time.

They can teach you what *not* to do.

The Miracle of Cassettes

When I started on the tour, the only way to hear a speaker was to *go* to hear him speak. It was time-consuming and expensive. No longer.

Now, thanks to the invention of the cassette recorder, it's possible to hear almost *any* speaker, anytime, at very low cost. So I urge you to build your own cassette library.

Some of the best sources of cassette tapes are:

Bureau of Business Practice
(Div. of Prentice-Hall)
Waterford, Connecticut 06385

General Cassette Corporation
1324 North 22nd Avenue
Phoenix, Arizona 85005

Nightingale-Conant Organization
3730 West Devon Avenue
Chicago, Illinois 60659

Success Motivation Institute
Waco, Texas 76710

Travel & Leisure, the American Express magazine, points out that there are some 20,000 different cassettes available from these and other organizations. Many are "live," so you can get the true feel of the audience.

Cassettes truly do work miracles!

How to Learn by Doing

Several decades ago, when Bill Gove first aspired to success on the platform, he heard the then-great—and still-great—Dr. Kenneth McFarland, surely the dean of American speakers.

As Bill tells it, he rushed over to Dr. McFarland following the meeting, and asked how *he* might become a great speaker, also.

Ken McFarland's answer: "If you want to speak, *speak!*"

Good advice!

No book (even this one!), no cassette, no course can take the place of actual "live" experience. In public speaking, as in most other endeavors, you learn by *doing*.

So speak at every opportunity.

If your company is planning a meeting, try to get on the program. If you belong to a Rotary Club, Kiwanis, or other similar organization, join some committees. Become active in your church, P.T.A., United Fund, or whatever. All provide excellent opportunities to speak.

Similarly, if you can work up a talk that's of general interest, let Rotary Clubs and others *know* about it. Organizations everywhere are constantly seeking speakers.

As I've mentioned repeatedly, such appearances build your prestige and income in many ways—as well as improving your own Miracle Platform Power.

And, obviously, the more you improve, the more you'll enjoy doing it.

And remember: It's important to do it *often*. Speaking is not like bicycle-riding. Over a period of time, you *do* forget how—or, at least, you get rusty.

The great piano virtuoso, Ignatz Paderewski, once said: "If I skip practice for a day, I notice it; if I skip practice for two days, the critics notice it; if I skip practice for three days, the audience notices it!"

Again, we learn a thing by doing it—and doing it *repeatedly*.

Remember Your Responsibility

Since this book deals primarily with speaking *techniques*— not necessarily speeches—little has been mentioned about *what* we say. Only how we say it. But, perhaps we should think for just a moment about the *subject matter* of our talks also.

Our ability, as speakers, gives you and me what may be the greatest power on earth. We strongly influence the thoughts and actions of our listeners—and, by so doing, we can literally transform people's lives.

So, it seems to me, it's up to us to change those lives for the better.

To build people up, not tear them down.

To add joy, not sorrow.

To foster good, not bad.

And, finally, to practice what we preach to the maximum.

Remember, one of the greatest stem-winders of all time was a flamboyant man named Adolf Hitler. But, a far greater orator was a very simple man named Jesus of Nazareth.

Let's decide, you and I, to emulate the latter.

A Final Encore

Now, let me tell you something about Lou Little's tear-jerker in Chapter 10.

I've been telling that story for over ten years. I've told it many hundreds of times. People tell me I do it pretty well.

But even now, writing this in my den at home, some tears have fallen. They always do. I mean it. That story gets me.

And I hope it gets you.

Because it carries a message for us as speakers, too. In our field, as in any other, the "overnight successes" are almost invariably the people who *worked* at it. They *became* "overnight successes" after ten or twenty years.

And, when you think of it, in speaking or in anything else, none of us is "born" that much better than the other. Mostly, some of us just work harder.

It's like a horse-race, with three horses charging down the home stretch. Maybe they're neck and neck, maybe there's a photo finish. But *one horse wins* — and wins, say, $100,000.

The second horse lost by a whisker and wins, say, $50,000.

And the third horse—who only lost by an inch—wins maybe $10,000.

Is the first horse ten times better than the third horse? Of course not. He's just got that slight *competitive edge* that makes the difference. *There's* the real miracle!

And that, in the last analysis, is what I earnestly hope this book may have given you.

Neither you nor I can ask for more.

MIRACLE PLATFORM POWER CAPSULE

1) Improvement is a never-ending process:
   When you stop getting better, you stop being good.
2) Watch the experts:
   You can always learn from a pro.
3) Build a cassette library:
   Then you can improve anywhere, anytime.
4) Speak wherever you can, as often as you can:
   We all learn by doing.
5) Remember your responsibility:
   What you say is important, too.
6) The final encore:
   All you need is a slight competitive edge—if you USE IT!

12

Ready-Reference Story-Teller's Guide

Here now, as promised, are some sure-fire audience-tested jokes, stories and gags you can use to liven up any speech.

They're listed by subject for easy use, and many have lead-in lines to help you fit them into your talk.

One important word in this connection:

There are many talented writers who "create" comedy material for speakers and entertainers. Much of it is excellent. But a lot of it isn't.

So in preparing this special section of the book, I went straight to those who *know* what works and what doesn't—*the best speakers in America.*

Please bear in mind, also, that this is not *my* evaluation. At the most recent convention of the National Speakers Association, this professional organization designated the few platform pros—

among all speakers everywhere—who merit the coveted C.P.A.E. award as the very finest speakers in the country.

The material that follows was contributed exclusively by these proven pros.

My deep thanks to all.

The C.P.A.E. speakers who have contributed to this section are, alphabetically:

Ty Boyd   Jim Newman
Alan Cimberg   Ken Olson
Sam Edwards   Nido Qubein
Bill Gove   Cavett Robert
Tennyson Guyer   Arthur Secord
Tom Haggai   Lewis Timberlake
Roy Hatten   Herb True
Ira Hayes   Charley Willey
Christopher Hegarty   Heartsill Wilson
Don Hutson   Carl Winters
Charles Jarvis   John Wolfe
Kenneth McFarland   Dave Yoho
Arthur H. "Red" Motley

ACTION

Thinking about something is not enough—you've got to take some action.

I know a guy who gets up every day, sings in the shower, plays an inspirational recording at breakfast, looks in the mirror with confidence and gives himself a rousing pep talk every morning: "You *can* do it . . . you *can* do it! What the mind of man can conceive, it can achieve!" and so on.

His only problem? The bum never leaves the house!

ACTORS

The old actor hadn't had a part in anything for a long, long time. He still dreamed of returning to the exciting stage, but the years were running out on him.

One night, he got a call from an agent telling him they needed a man urgently to fill in for an actor who had been unexpectedly taken ill. "The show opens tomorrow night," the agent said.

"Gosh, I can't learn a whole part in one day," lamented the old actor.

"Nothing to it. Your only line is:'Hark the cannon.' Practice it, and be at the theater at 7:00 P.M."

So next day, all day long, the old actor rehearsed his line trying to find just the right inflection, the right delivery.

"Hark THE cannon."

"HARK the cannon."

"Hark the CANNON!"

That night he arrived at the theater. They dressed him in his costume.

"Come on, we're late," the stage manager shouted.

"You're on, you're on," they screamed as they pushed him out of the wings on to the stage.

He'd no sooner hit the stage when this tremendous roar of a cannon rolled out across the theater.

Stunned, the old actor in complete shock hollered: "What the hell was *that?*"

ADULT LITERATURE

"What are your views on pornography?"
"Oh, about 20-20!"

* * * * *

I subscribe to Playboy for the same reason I subscribe to the National Geographic: I just love to look at the colorful pictures of all the lovely places I ain't never going to get to!

ADVICE

I'm not here to preach to you or give you advice—there's too much of that going on, anyway.

Two fellows became great buddies because they had something in common—each had a little physical affliction. One stammered, and the other had one foot shorter than the other.

So the guy who stammered said to his friend: "S-s-s-ay, I g-g-g-ot a g-g-g-great idea for you. Why don't you w-w-w-walk along the street with one f-f-f-foot in the gutter?"

The other fellow thought this was a great idea so he tried it—and it worked fine! He was waltzing along the street doing just great—till he came to the end of the block, then he fell down and was run over by a bus.

A week later, he's in the hospital, bandaged from head to foot, and the friend comes in to see him.

"Gee, I'm s-s-s-sorry, I g-g-g-guess my advice w-w-w-wasn't so good!"

The other fellow said: "No, it sure wasn't. But I've got a solution for *your* problem, Buster: Keep your darn mouth shut!"

AMERICA

America is the only country in the world where you can see a Priest drinking Mogen David wine, out of a Mason jar.

* * * * *

America is the only place where kids sing about "getting back to the simple life"—accompanied by their $3000 sound system.

* * * * *

And America is the only country where a Johnny Cash could make two million dollars a year, just singing about "Hard Times."

APPLICATIONS

Some of the things you see on applications today—they're really something!

I saw one that a guy filled out for a job as a staff manager—he wasn't too bright.

Under "Age" he put "Atomic."

Under "Race" he put "human."

Under "Church preference"—"red brick colonial with white trim."

And under "marital status"—"shaky."
"Salary desired"—"yes."
"Born"—"Caesarean section!"

ARGUMENTS

Two cars banged into each other. "What's the matter with ya?
Are you blind?" the first driver yelled.

The other promptly countered, "Blind? I hit ya, didn't I?"

ARMED SERVICES

A guy was taking his Army physical.

The psychiatrist said: "Why do you want to go into the
Service?"

The fellow said: "Because I *hate* the enemy! I'll fight 'em with
everything I've got! I'll shoot 'em with my gun, spear 'em with my
bayonet, and chop 'em up with my pocket knife. And if I lose all my
weapons, I'll *bite* 'em!"

You'll *what?*" asked the doctor.

"I'll *bite* 'em!"

"You know, you're a little nuts," the shrink said.

"Put it down, Doc, put it down!"

BARS

The connoisseur sat down at the bar and ordered a martini.
"Very dry," he insisted. "Twenty parts gin to one part vermouth."

"All right, sir," said the bartender. "Shall I twist a bit of lemon
peel over it?"

"My good man, when I want lemonade, I'll ask for it."

*   *   *   *   *

"Will you have a drink?" the young man asked.

"I don't drink," his date replied.

"May I offer you a cigarette?"

"I don't smoke," she said.

"Would you be interested in going up to my apartment, putting a little mood music on the phonograph and . . ." She answered by slapping his face.

"I don't suppose you eat hay either," he said, nursing his jaw.

"Well, hardly," she said icily.

"Just as I thought," he sighed. "Not fit company for man or beast."

*　*　*　*　*

A drunk staggered into a bar and said to the bartender: "Set up the whole house." The bartender gave everyone a drink and handed the check to the drunk.

"Golly, bartender—I can't find my wallet."

The bartender grabbed the drunk and threw him right out of the place. A couple of weeks later the same drunk came staggering in again.

"Gimme a drink and set up the house," he shouted. "But not you, bartender. You get mean when you drink."

*　*　*　*　*

A kangaroo walked into a bar, sat down on a stool and said to the bartender: "Gimme a martini."

The shocked bartender served the kangaroo the martini, walked over to the owner of the bar and said: "Hey, boss, would you believe it! A kangaroo just came in and ordered a martini. We can't have animals in here drinking, it will ruin our business."

"Tell you what to do," said the owner. "Go over and charge him $5 for the drink."

After presenting the bill to the kangaroo, the bartender casually said to him: "We don't see many kangaroos in here."

The kangaroo looked at the check, looked up at the bartender and said: "Buddy, at these prices—you ain't *going* to see many kangaroos in here!"

*　*　*　*　*

This fellow went into a bar with a little dog. They sat down and the bartender came over and said: "Hey, get that mutt out of here!"

"He's not going to hurt anyone," answered the customer. "I'm going to have a beer, and he and I are going to chat a little."

"A talking dog!" roared the bartender. "You think I'm an imbecile? Dogs can't talk!"

"Oh yes he can. In fact, he can read."

"I've got $20 that says he can't."

"O.K. I'll just bet you he can," said the customer. And with that he gave the dog 75 cents and told him to go over to the cigarette machine and get a pack of Winstons. "With all those different brands he'd have to be able to read, wouldn't he, to know which were Winstons?"

The bartender agreed and the dog trotted off. However, instead of going to the cigarette machine he zipped out the door and was gone.

"Wow," said the customer, "let's find him. He's a very valuable dog."

They searched all over the neighborhood but to no avail.

Several hours later in comes the dog. He's saturated with perspiration, panting and beat. Right behind him is a cute little female dog also in a state of tired collapse.

"You miserable dog," hollered the owner, "in all the years I've had you you've never done anything like this before!"

The tired dog looked up at him, almost smiling, and said: "Buddy, this is the first time I ever had the money to do anything like this!"

*   *   *   *   *

A man walks into a bar with a little dog. They sit down and the bartender walks over, looks at the dog, turns to the man and says: "Get that dog out of here. We don't allow animals in this bar."

"He won't bother anyone," replied the owner. "We're just going to sit here and talk quietly."

"Talk!" roared the bartender. "Dogs can't talk. You think I'm an idiot, telling me you're going to talk?"

"Well, he certainly *can* talk. In fact, not only can he talk but he can even recite the Gettysburg Address."

"Look buddy," answered the taken-aback bartender. "I've

got $10 that says that dog can't even say his name, let alone the Gettysburg Address."

Quickly, several other people overhearing the conversation jumped at the opportunity to get in on a good deal.

"I'll take 5 bucks on that."

"Give me $20. He won't do it." and so on.

Soon the bar was stacked with money.

"O.K., Rover," said his owner, "recite the Gettysburg Address."

The dog just sat there.

"Go on," the owner urged, "say it."

Nothing.

Everyone roared with laughter, picked up the money, and the man and his dog quietly walked out of the bar.

Once outside, the guy tore into his dog, slapping him across the face. "You dirty dog, I spend months teaching you how to talk. I teach you the Gettysburg Address. We finally have the stage all set to make a quick killing for a pile of dough and you louse it up. You nutty or something?"

"Course I'm not nutty," answered the dog. "You're the stupid one. What do you think the odds are going to be the next time we go in that bar?"

* * * * *

A customer at the bar was getting drunker and noisier until the bartender had to warn him to quiet down.

"Don't be fussy," said the customer, "this is my 30th wedding anniversary."

"Oh, well," said the bartender, "go ahead and enjoy yourself. That certainly calls for a celebration!"

"No, you don't understand," said the customer. "I'm not celebrating. I'm drowning my sorrows."

"Whatever for?" asked the bartender.

"Well, you see, after I was married five years, I was ready to murder my wife. But my lawyer was a friend and he persuaded me not to. He said the least I could get was 25 years in jail. And I was foolish enough to listen to him. Think of it! If I'd gone ahead with it, I'd be a free man today!"

* * * * *

A grasshopper walked into a tavern and hopped up on the bar stool. "I'll have a scotch and soda."

The bartender said: "Did you know we have a drink named after you?"

"Really, you mean you have a drink named 'Irving'?" asked the grasshopper.

BILLS

Memo from credit department: "Your account has been on our books for over a year and we would like to remind you that we have now carried you longer than your mother did."

BIRTHDAYS

A fellow called his friend on the phone and said: "Charlie, tomorrow's my birthday, and we're having a little party at the house. We want you to come. It's nothing fancy, so don't stand on ceremony. Don't dress up, just come on over after work, ring the doorbell with your elbow, and come on in."

The friend said: "Fine! But why ring the doorbell with my *elbow*?"

"Hell, Man, it's my birthday. You're not coming *empty-handed*, are you?"

BUSINESS

There was a polite bank robber who walked into the bank with pistol drawn and said: "Ladies and Gentlemen, those in favor of leaving these premises alive will kindly hold up their hands."

* * * * *

Did you hear about the auto mechanic who bought a hospital and is making a fortune? You take your wife in for an operation and they give you a loaner.

* * * * *

Doing business without advertising is like winking at a girl in the dark; you know what you're doing, but nobody else does.

* * * * *

"What's wrong with the computer?" the office manager asked.

"Someone dropped a rubber band in it and now it's making snap decisions."

* * * * *

With acupuncture becoming so popular, there may soon be a Mao Clinic.

* * * * *

He wanted to do a little remodeling and called in a housepainter for an estimate. The painter said he'd take the job for seven hundred dollars.

"Seven hundred dollars!" cried the outraged homeowner. "Why, I wouldn't pay Van Gogh that much."

"Oh, yeah?" replied the painter. "If he does the job for any less, he'll have to cross a picket line first."

* * * * *

While cleaning out some desk drawers, a man found an old shoe repair ticket. To the best of his recollection, he couldn't remember the shoes. It must have been several years ago that he had gotten this ticket.

Anyway, he stuck the ticket in his pocket, and that night on the way home from work, he stopped at this shoe repair shop. He walked up to the counter, handed the ticket to the old shoemaker and didn't say a word.

The old gentleman studied the ticket for several minutes, walked into the back room, came out, and with a slight nod to the customer, said: "They'll be ready next Tuesday!"

* * * * *

My accountant had a clever idea. He told me to send in my estimated tax without signing it.

They want me to guess how much I'm going to earn; so, let them guess who sent it in.

CAPITALISM

During a Russian visitor's tour of an automobile factory, he stopped to chat with a worker. "Why," he asked, "do you prefer the capitalistic system to the communistic system?"

"Let me explain," said the worker, drawing a deep breath. "Say it's about quitting time and you're standing on the corner waiting for a bus and a big black limousine comes along. It stops in front of you, and you see it's your boss. He tells you to hop in and you drive away. He says, 'How about coming to my estate for a swim?' so you go, and when you finish he serves you a tall cool drink, and invites you to stay for dinner, and a few more tall cool drinks, and the boss suggests you stay overnight. You do, and after a delicious breakfast, you drive back to the factory with the boss. That is why I like capitalism."

"Good heavens," gasped the astonished Russian, "has that happened to you?"

"No," admitted the worker, "but it's happened to my sister twice."

*   *   *   *   *

Socialism is when you have two cows and give one to your neighbor.

Communism is when you have two cows but the government takes both and gives you the milk.

Capitalism is when you have two cows. You sell one and buy a bull. That's free enterprise.

*   *   *   *   *

A man was driving through his suburban home area one morning and was amused by seeing a youngster sitting by the side of the road. He had a little dog on his lap and a crudely lettered sign stuck in the ground and tied on a little tree branch. The sign boldly announced, "Dog For Sale."

The man stopped, rolled down the window, and asked the youngster, "How much do you want for your puppy?"

"$50,000," answered the little boy.

The man smiled and drove away.

Later the same day the man was returning home and again passed the place where the little boy had been sitting. The dog was gone and the little boy was having fun playing with some other youngsters. The man stopped and called to him. "Hey, son, did you sell your dog?"

"Oh, yes," replied the boy.

"Did you get $50,000?"

"Well, in a way. I traded him for two $25,000 cats plus a dime, so I really made a little profit!"

COINCIDENCE

Success in life is never a coincidence.

Like the three fellows who showed up at the Pearly Gates at precisely the same moment. St. Peter was astounded to see these three guys there at exactly the same time, he was amazed, so he said: "Are you fellows friends—are you together or something?"

They said, "No."

St. Peter said, "Well, that's an amazing coincidence—all of you showing up here at the same instant—I'd like to know how come." So he asked the first fellow: "What happened to you?"

The guy said, "Well, you see, I've been a business man, living in New York, in a high-rise apartment, and I've been taking a lot of trips. I came back from one trip a couple of days early—it was about noon—and I went up to the apartment, opened the door, and I found two martinis on the coffee table and a cigar butt in the ashtray, so I got suspicious. I looked all through the apartment, couldn't find anyone else, and suddenly I remembered that the floor below had a terrace. I looked out onto that terrace, and there to my horror was a guy in his shorts! So with rage and indignation, I stormed into the kitchen, picked up the refrigerator, and somehow managed to lug it through the living room to that window. And, with a mighty heave, I tossed it onto that terrace. But, just at that moment, I was overcome with a heart attack."

St. Peter said, "Well, I can see how that might happen." He turned to the second man and said: "What happened to you?"

"Well," he said, "I've been a business man, living in a high-rise apartment in New York, and we happened to have a terrace. Every noon I liked to take a sun bath in my shorts, and all of a sudden I got hit on the head with a refrigerator!"

St. Peter said, "Well, I guess that could happen." He turned to the third fellow and said: "What happened to *you*?"

He said, "Darned if I know. I was just minding my own business, sitting there in a refrigerator!"

COMPOSURE

Sometimes we have to *work* at composure.

A man walked into a supermarket with his 18-month-old son, and put the infant in a shopping cart as he did his shopping. As things happen, the kid started to bawl at the top of his lungs.

The man kept saying, calmly: "Don't get upset, Albert. Please, Albert. Don't make a fuss, Albert."

A lady, seeing this, complimented the man: "I can't help admiring the way you speak to your child."

"You've got it backwards, Lady," he said: "*I'm* Albert!"

COMPUTERS

Computers are pretty complicated gadgets—especially if you don't know much about them.

A quiet old janitor was going about his duties one night, cleaning up in the data processing company offices. The shrill ring of the phone snapped him to attention. Being the only person there, he timidly lifted the receiver and softly said: "Hello."

A very disturbed individual shrieked at him over the phone— a tirade of problems about tape drive being down, memory units not working, and a long list of other very technical complaints. It ended with the caller's demand to know: "What can you do to help me right now?"

"Sir," the old janitor answered softly, "when I said 'hello' I told you all I know about this computer business!"

CONSULTANTS

I'm a sales consultant. People ask me what that means, and the best way I know to describe it is to tell you about this tomcat we had—a real hell-raiser.

He was out every night—every night all over town, raising hell. So we finally had him fixed.

Now he just goes out occasionally as a consultant.

CONVENTIONS

The executive, attending a convention, had just finished eating in the restaurant and had returned to his room. He was startled when he walked into the room to find two sexy-looking girls inside. He immediately cried out: "You girls are interlopers! I'm a married man, a pillar of my church, and scandal has never touched my personal deportment. So, *one* of you girls will have to go!"

*   *   *   *   *

Funeral directors have conventions, too.

At one such affair, the boys were whooping it up one night—as happens at all conventions—and several practical jokers locked up one of their buddies in a casket, to sleep it off.

The next morning he woke up—with a slight hangover, but still a logical mind—and reasoned things out.

"Either I'm dead or I'm alive," he said to himself.

"If I'm alive, what am I doing here?

"But if I'm dead, why do I have to go to the men's room?"

COOPERATION

It's tough to get people to cooperate.

A minister was talking to his group, his flock, urging them to become more active in church affairs, to take part, to participate, to get the church moving again.

"Brothers and Sisters, we is stale-mated, that's what. We need for this church to get up and *move*. This church has got to get up and walk."

A voice from the rear of the church hollered: "Let 'er walk, Brother, let 'er walk!"

The minister continued: "Not only we got to get up and walk, we got to run."

Same voice in the back: "Let 'er run, Brother, let 'er run!"

"And not only we got to walk, not only we got to run, but this here church is going to have to fly."

"Let 'er fly, Brother, let 'er fly!"

"Now, wait a minute back there, Brother. *Flying* is another thing. Flying takes sacrifice. And that means that everyone in here got to sacrifice—with his time and with his money."

The shout came back: "Let 'er walk, Brother, let 'er walk!"

CUSTOMERS

Customer to car salesman: "You told me how good a car this was when you sold it to me three months ago. Now tell me all over again; I'm getting discouraged."

DEFINITIONS

Arthritis: Twinges in the hinges.

Atheist: A man who has no invisible means of support.

College bred: A 4-year loaf made with father's dough.

Egomaniac: A person who doesn't go around talking about other people.

Faith: Something you believe in when you don't have anything to believe in.

Humility: Exemplified by the person who has a Rolls Royce, a Mercedes, a Maserati, and a Ferrari. When someone asks him, "George, which car did you bring today?" he replies, "The green one."

Lawyers: The only people I know who can write a 10,000 word document and call it a brief.

Minute Man: One who can make it to the refrigerator and back while the commercial is on.

Naturalist: A guy who throws sevens.

Opera: Where a guy gets stabbed in the back, but instead of bleeding he sings.

Summer Camp: Where parents spend $1,000 so their daughter can learn to make a 50 cent potholder.

DEPRESSION

Things are tough today; it's easy to get depressed.

One fellow was standing on the edge of the Golden Gate Bridge, about to jump. A passerby stopped to comfort him and keep him from committing suicide. So they sat by the edge of the bridge and talked. Ten minutes later, they both jumped!

DESIRES

Sometimes, there are things you just have to do.

If you ever have the occasion to fly west out of Denver, Colorado, chances are that you will fly over a range known as the

Collegiate Mountains. Nestled immediately behind these beautiful snow-capped peaks is a valley—a valley that at one time in history was the center of the silver-mining rush—and the only city in that valley was Tin Cup, Colorado, now nothing more than a small settlement, bordering on a ghost town.

History tells us that on one bright sunny Saturday morning, in the midst of the boomtown atmosphere, a bearded, shabby and aged prospector came into the town to replenish his supply of coffee, sugar, flour and salt. As he hitched his mule Annie and the small wagon at the hitching rail in front of the saloon, he was confronted by an Eastern dude—a brash young rookie with a white hat, polished boots and a neckerchief tied around his neck.

This young creature confronted the aging prospector, blocking his progress toward the saloon, and demanded: "Dance a jig for the people!"

"Why, I ain't never danced a step in my life, son," the prospector responded in a nervous and confused voice.

"Well, old timer, you'd better learn fast, 'cause this six-gun is gonna teach you in a hurry!" And with the threat heard by all the bystanders, the dude began to fire into the dusty street around the worn-out boots of the prospector—until the sixth bullet was expended into the sand around the old man.

When the last shot echoed up and down the crowded street, a faint smile began to emerge on the face of the old prospector. Slowly he turned, reached into his little wagon, and came forth with his trusty Winchester rifle. He injected a single shell into the breech, gazed at the rear end of Annie the mule, and then up to the puzzled expression on the Eastern dude's face.

Then he calmly asked: "Son, have you ever *kissed a mule?*"

The bewildered and frightened young dude looked at the stern and resolute face of the old prospector—then down to the trusty Winchester resting across the miner's arm—and lastly to the projected rear end of Annie, who was nonchalantly flicking away the flies with her bushy tail . . . and responded, "No, sir. I don't guess that I've ever kissed a mule before in my life. But I want you to know . . . in the last few moments *I've developed an un-controllable urge to do so.*"

* * * * *

You have to find out what people *want and desire.*

A priest was calling on a drunk in a flop-house. There he was—the drunk—lying on this dirty cot, in this dingy room; and in the corner of the room, in a cage, was a parrot.

The parrot kept saying, "Hey, how about it? Hey, how about it?"

The priest said to the man, "You're really in deep trouble, friend. Not only are you a drunken bum, but that bird is a juvenile delinquent! But, fortunately for you, I also own a parrot. Sweetest parrot you ever saw—she just sits there all day long and prays. So next week I'm going to come back and see you, and I'll bring my parrot along. We'll put the two parrots together, and it'll have a beautiful effect."

So, the next week, the priest came back and, sure enough, he had his parrot perched on his shoulder. She was just sitting there, wings pressed together, praying.

They got inside the room and the drunk's parrot said: "Hey, how about it? Hey, how about it?"

The priest's parrot threw open her arms and said: "Thank God! My prayers are answered!"

DIETS

I tried the seven-day diet, and I lost a week.

* * * * *

Then I tried the drinking man's diet—now I've got *two* problems.

DISCIPLINE

Discipline is such a part of our lives, yet none of us really like it. We talk about our kids repudiating and refuting discipline—there's nothing new about that. We all do it all the time, and have all of our lives. *Discipline* is seldom *pleasant.* I happen to believe that today's generation of young people is the finest the world has ever produced and their confrontation with imposed *discipline* is no different to them than our discipline is to us, and we don't like it because it impinges upon us. I think I can prove it.

You remember that night you were parked out along the country road and the police car came by and stopped?—and the policeman got out with his flashlight and shined it in the window of your car. You didn't like him very well that night, did you? You didn't like policemen in general very well that night, did you? You weren't at that very moment the greatest proponent of law and order the world had ever known, but two nights later you heard a noise out in the garage and you called the police department and that *same* policeman, in that *same* police car with that *same* flashlight came up and saved you—again!!!

DOCTORS

A doctor calls a plumber at 4:00 a.m. and says, "You've got to get over here. My toilet's leaking!"

The plumber says, "But, Doc, it's 4:00 o'clock in the morning!"

"I know it's 4 o'clock," says the Doctor. "I can tell time. But stuff is running all over my living room! And *you* call *me* at all hours!"

"O.K., Doc," says the plumber. "Drop three aspirin in the bowl, flush it, and call me back at 10:00 a.m."

* * * * *

A guy goes to a psychiatrist and says: "I can't go to sleep at night. Little animals are running up and down my bed. What should I do?"

Psychiatrist: "For $50 I will cure it."

Patient: "That crazy I'm not. I will find someone else."

Six months later, the psychiatrist meets him again and says, "How is your problem?"

Patient: "I solved it."

Psychiatrist: "How, another psychiatrist?"

Patient: "No, I went to my brother."

Psychiatrist: "Is he a psychiatrist?"

Patient: "No, he is a carpenter."

Psychiatrist: "What did he do?"

Patient: "He cut off the legs of the bed."

* * * * *

A doctor had three little boys in his waiting room, waiting for polio shots.

He went to the first little boy, who was reading Popular Mechanics, and said: "What do you want to be when you grow up?"

The kid said: "I want to be an engineer—to fix cars and make airplanes fly."

The second kid, who was reading Field and Stream, said in answer to the same question: "I want to be a guide and take people where the fish bite and the big game hide."

The third kid was asked the same question—"What do you want to be when *you* grow up?"

Looking up from a copy of Playboy, he said: "I don't know what you call it. But I can't wait to get started!"

DRUNKS

The drunk was having a great day at the circus. He was taking in every show and liberally enjoying the cold flowing beer. In fact, by afternoon he was pretty well bombed.

He stumbled into a side show. At that moment they were in the process of having a beautiful girl in a tiny bikini jump into a cage with a wild, ferocious lion.

The drunk was terrified to see the lion lunge at this beautiful girl. But she quickly side-stepped the lion, and they went round and round; the girl talking to the lion, quieting him down. Pretty soon they were walking around, then standing still, then sitting down, and the girl was patting the lion's head. Finally, the girl stretched out on the floor on her back. The lion licked her on her ankle, then her thigh, her stomach, her . . . . The drunk can't believe what he's seeing. As he sways back and forth in his alcoholic stupor, another man standing next to him, looks at him, sees his condition and his intense involvement. He says humorously to the drunk: "That's pretty neat, isn't it?"

"You're darn right that's neat. That's terrific!"

"You think you could get in there and do that?" asks the man.

"Hell, I know damn well I can—if they get that lion out of there!"

*   *   *   *   *

"Henry, you are drunk," said his wife as they waited for the parking lot attendant to bring them their car. "Don't you know why they say, 'Don't drink when you drive'?"

"I sure do," said Henry. "You might hit a bump and spill some."

*   *   *   *   *

Two drunks accidentally wandered into an amusement park and boarded a roller coaster. The ride was fast and furious, but it didn't seem to make much of an impression. As they were getting off, one drunk was heard to say, "You know, we may have made good time, but I have a feeling we took the wrong bus."

*   *   *   *   *

I said to a guy: "Does your tongue burn when you drink?"

"I don't know. I never got drunk enough to light it."

*   *   *   *   *

Then there was the drunk who called the hotel manager at 8:00 a.m., saying, "Shay, what time does the bar open?"

"11:00 a.m.," came the reply.

A few minutes later: "Shay, Buddy, what time does the bar open?"

"I just told you, Sir. 11:00 o'clock."

Another minute later: "Shay, Buddy, what time does the bar open?"

"I *told* you, Sir. 11:00 o'clock. You'll just have to wait till then to go in."

"Who wants to get in? I want to get *out!*"

*   *   *   *   *

A drunk, riding in a bus, is tearing up a newspaper into little scraps of paper and throwing them out the window.

The woman sitting next to him asks: "What in the world are you doing that for?"

"To scare away the elephants," he says.

"But there aren't any elephants around here," she says, smiling.

"See! It works!"

FASTIDIOUSNESS

It's important to be well groomed—but that can be overdone, too.

I knew a fella who was *too* fastidious—always straightening his tie, slicking back his hair—they called him Spotless Harry.

One day, he was walking down the street and met an old friend.

"Harry!" the friend said. "Spotless Harry! How've you been?"

"Oh, I've been all right," Harry said, straightening his tie. "I got married a couple of months ago."

"Gee, that's a great, Harry! Did you go on a honeymoon?"

"Of course I went on a honeymoon," Harry said, slicking back his hair. "That's the usual procedure, isn't it?"

"Gee, I'm glad to hear that, Harry! On your honeymoon, did you—you know—sleep with your wife?"

"Of course! I married the girl, didn't I?" said Harry, flicking an invisible spot off his trousers.

"Just one more question, Harry: Did you—you know—get your wife *pregnant*?"

"God, I hope so," said Harry. "I sure wouldn't want to go through *that* messy thing again!"

FLYING

One of the airlines recently introduced a special half-fare rate for wives accompanying their husbands on business trips. Anticipating some valuable testimonials, the publicity department of the airline sent out letters to all the wives of businessmen who used the special rates, asking how they enjoyed their trip.

Responses are still pouring in asking, "What trip?"

*   *   *   *   *

The jet-liner was on routine flight but had run into a sudden violent storm. A nice old lady appealed to the minister sitting next to her.

"Please," she said, "I think we're going to crash. Can't you do something to save us?"

"I'm terribly sorry," said the minister, calmly, "but there's not much I can do. You see, I'm in sales, not management!"

*   *   *   *   *

I flew in here on a 747. That's a big airplane! They have 400 passengers and three rest rooms. That's what's known as a holding pattern!

*   *   *   *   *

The worst thing about flying is going through the Dallas airport. Biggest in the world—bigger than Manhattan Island—and the problems they have with people getting lost is unbelievable.

Last week I came through that airport, and while I was talking with the ticket agent a young lady rushed up who was quite obviously in a very maternal way.

She grabbed the agent by the lapel and shouted, "Get me out of this airport, I'm going to have a baby!"

He answered, "Honey, I can't get you out of this airport; you shouldn't have come in here in that condition!"

She said, "When I came in here, I wasn't even married!"

*   *   *   *   *

Before landing, the pilot called the tower and said: "I need a time check; what time is it?"

The guy in the tower said: "Well, if you're United Air Lines, it's 1700 Greenwich; if you're Braniff, it's 5:00 p.m.; but if you're Texas International, the big hand is on the 12 and the little hand is on the 5!"

FOOTBALL

The head football coach gathered his pro team around him for the opening coaching session. "I know that you have all had many years of football experience," he said, "but a review of basic fundamentals is good for everyone now and then."

The coach picked up a football, held it over his head. "Let's start at the beginning. This is a football," he said, extending the ball towards the group. "We play this game on a field which is 100 yards long."

At this point a voice from the back row was heard. "Wait a minute, coach, you're going too fast!"

*   *   *   *   *

I asked a pro football player which he preferred, grass or astroturf. He said: "Dunno—I never smoked astroturf."

*   *   *   *   *

But coaches have a tough time. This college alumnus was chewing out the coach. "How many kids do you have in this school?"

"Oh, about 4000," said the coach.

"Would it be too much to have two of 'em out in front of the ball carrier next Saturday?"

*   *   *   *   *

In Houston we have some real losers—like the Oilers. I'm just waiting for 'em to win the *toss* some time!

*   *   *   *   *

A referee was pacing off a penalty. "You *stink!*" said the offending player.

"5, 10, 15 . . . how do I smell from here?"

GAMBLING

"The trouble with Vegas is it gets so monotonous watching those beautiful girls dancing around on stage, and then wasting time drinking martinis and gambling . . . and let me tell you something else my wife said the other day . . ."

* * * * *

A guy went broke at the tables in Vegas. He met a friend, borrowed $20 and lost it. Then borrowed $50 from him, which he blew. Hit him once more and got $100 with the advice: "Take this and get a bus and go home."

But the fellow couldn't resist playing at the crap table again, only to lose the $100. He went into the men's room and told the attendant what had happened. The attendant advised: "There is only one thing to do, tap your friend once more." "Oh no, I won't do that. That guy's bad luck!"

* * * * *

The stranger walked up to a Las Vegas dice table and laid down a $1000 bet. He shook the dice, but as he threw them a third cube fell unexpectedly from his sleeve. The house operator was unruffled. He handed back two of the dice and pocketed the third, saying, "OK, roll again. Your point is 16!"

* * * * *

Just got back from Vegas. Went there for a change and a rest. The slot machines got the change and the crap tables got the rest.

GLASSES

It's quite a shock getting your first pair of bifocals. You look down and you have the same problem as Raquel Welch. You can't see your feet.

*   *   *   *

A man visited his optometrist to have his glasses checked. "They just aren't strong enough," he told the doctor. "Don't you have something stronger?"

"Yes," said the optometrist, "there is one lens that is stronger."

"Just one?" asked the man. "What comes after that?"

"After that," the doctor said, "you buy a dog."

GOLF

A guy is playing golf with his wife, and she has a stroke. He carries her all the way into the clubhouse.

The pro says: "What a magnificent display of energy! She weighs about 165 pounds—you're only about 140. And you carried her all the way in!"

"It wasn't the carrying that was so tough," the guy answers. "It was the picking her up and putting her down between shots!"

*   *   *   *

The golfer confidently eyed the next hole and remarked to his caddy: "This should be good for a long drive and a putt." His swing, however, hit the sod and pushed the ball only a few feet.

"Now," said the caddy, "for a hell of a putt."

*   *   *   *

I'm now playing with a senior golf group called the "Golden Oldies." You gotta be careful putting your glass down at a cocktail party, though. Somebody will put his teeth in it.

*   *   *   *

A golfer at a 19th hole bar, said to his playing partner, "My wife told me this morning that she is going to leave me if I don't give up playing golf. I'm certainly going to miss her!"

GOVERNMENT

Interviewer to Congressman: "What do you think of the abortion bill?"

Congressman: "I think they ought to pay it."

* * * * *

They say that nothing's sure except death and taxes. But there's a difference: Death doesn't get any worse when Congress is in session.

* * * * *

They say that being in Congress is like having lockjaw and being seasick at the same time.

* * * * *

The three biggest white lies told in America:

1) Your check is in the mail.
2) I gave at the office.
3) I'm with the government; I'm here to help you.

INSURANCE

Prospect says: "Why should I buy life insurance? If I die, my wife will get all the money. She'll get married again, some guy'll move in and spend all my money."
Salesman: "Stop worrying. Maybe the second guy won't be a cheapskate like you!"

INTELLIGENCE

Horses are smart. You'll never see 'em betting on people.

* * * * *

And squirrels are smarter than people, too. You'll never see squirrels taking up a collection of nuts for other squirrels who won't work.

* * * * *

A man doesn't need to be brilliant to be successful.
I know a kid who flunked out of high school and immediately went out and made a million dollars.
He ran into his math prof some time later, and the math prof said: "I've got to hand it to you. You were always such a dunce in

school . . . now you're fantastically successful. How did that happen?"

The kid said: "Well, see, right after I left school, I found this product that I could buy for $1 . . . and I could sell it for $5 . . . and I could sell all I could get. So I just kept doing it—buying it for one, selling it for five. I don't know how it works out, but somehow that little old *four per-cent* just keeps me going!"

JOKES

Some people are just funnier than others.

A new prisoner checked into San Quentin, and was amazed at what went on in the mess hall after dinner. One convict said: "349"—and everyone roared with laughter. Another said: "652"—and the place broke up. The new prisoner asked what was going on.

"Those are jokes," he was told. "We know them all so well after so many years, we give them numbers."

So the following night, during a lull in the festivities, the new prisoner shouted out: "781!" And nobody cracked a smile.

"That's the trouble," his cell-mate told him. "Some guys can tell jokes and some can't!"

KIDS

I come from a family of six kids. And we were poor, I mean *poor*. I never got to sleep alone until I was married!

But that isn't really true. Actually, while our own four youngsters all have their own beds they've always liked to crawl into the sack, at all hours of the night, to cuddle with Mommy and Daddy.

I finally decided to put a stop to this—to "wean" them, so to speak—so just before leaving on one trip, I gathered the family around the breakfast table and said: "Look, you kids all have your own beds. So from now on, let's meet *here* every morning. We'll expect you to stay in your own beds during the night, and not to bother us in our own room just as we'll not bother you in yours. And, same way, when Daddy is out of town, you're not to disturb Mother during the night."

When I came home from my trip a week later, the whole family met me at the airport.

Our little seven-year-old son rushed through the crowd and shouted at the top of his lungs: "Daddy, Daddy, guess what? The whole time you were gone, *nobody slept with Mommy!*"

* * * * *

A spinster schoolteacher took her fifth-grade charges on a field trip to a county fair. There was a race track on the grounds and she asked them whether they would enjoy seeing the horses. The children enthusiastically exclaimed they would, but as soon as she got them inside the gate, they all requested to be taken to the lavatory. She accompanied the little girls, but sent the boys to the men's room alone. They trooped out almost immediately and announced that the facilities were too high for them to reach.

The situation was an awkward one, but after looking about to make sure she was unobserved, the teacher ushered the boys back in. She lined them up before the plumbing and moved methodically down the line. After lifting several, she came to one who was unusually heavy.

"Goodness," she exclaimed, "are you in the fifth?"

"Hell no, lady," came the startled reply. "I'm riding Blue Grass in the third."

* * * * *

Little Johnnie came home from school and handed his father his report card. The father took one look and exploded. "Wow! Four E's and a D. How do you explain this?"

"Well, Dad, I guess I just spent too much time on one subject."

* * * * *

Two young boys were arguing.
"My father is better than your father!"
"No, he's not!"
"My brother is better than your brother!"
"No, he's not."
"My mother is better than your mother!"
"Well, I guess you've got me there. My father says the same thing."

* * * * *

Words are so important! I was telling our 6-year-old; "When you talk to the neighbors, just say that your aunt likes to crochet. Don't call her the happy hooker."

* * * * *

Conversation overheard involving 2 five-year-olds:
She: "Let's play pregnant."
He: "Okay, how do you play pregnant?"
She: "It's easy. We both go in the bathroom. You shave and I throw up."

LOSERS

A loser is a window-washer on the 17th floor with a kidney condition.

* * * * *

A loser is a guy who gets his junk mail postage due.

* * * * *

A loser is a girl who puts her bra on backwards—and it fits.

* * * * *

Now, I'm not saying I'm the *only* person who can do things. But I'm reminded of the two fellows who met at their college's tenth reunion. One was a 240-pound football player—he had to clench his fists to keep from walking on his hands! The other was a tiny little runt who may have weighed 90 pounds soaking wet. And they compared notes.

It seemed that both had gotten married immediately following graduation. But the big football player had remained childless, while the skinny little runt had sired ten bouncing baby boys.

So, the football player said, "I feel kinda silly asking *you* about these things—I was always the big man on campus and you were nothing—but I wonder if you can advise me: How can I procreate the race the way you have?"

The little guy said: "It's easy. When you get home from this reunion, just turn the lights down low, mix a pitcher of martinis and dance around the living room with your wife. Then, when you feel the moment is appropriate, just rip off her clothes and throw her down on the floor!"

"That sounds great! What do I do next?"

He said, "Send for me—send for me!"

LOVE

To love the world for me is no chore;
My only real problem is the neighbor next door.

*   *   *   *   *

A seven-year-old girl sent her father a beautiful fresh red rose with this note: "Dear Dad, this rose will soon fade and die; but you, Daddy, will smell forever."

*   *   *   *   *   *

"You always hurt the one you love," said the porcupine.

*   *   *   *   *

Gal: "Why do you love me? Is it my looks?"
Guy: "Nope."
Gal: "Is it my figure?"
Guy: "Nope."

Gal: "Is it my money?"
Guy: "Nope."
Gal: "I give up."
Guy: "That's the reason!"

MANIPULATION

A lobbyist who was opposing *any* large appropriation, approached a legislator who boasted of his self-education. "Do you realize," asked the lobbyist, gravely, "that up at the state college, men and women students have to use the same curriculum?"

The legislator looked startled.

"And that boys and girls often matriculate together?"

"No!" exclaimed the lawmaker.

The lobbyist came close and whispered, "And a young lady student can be forced at any time to show a male professor her thesis . . ."

The legislator shrank back in horror. "I won't vote 'em a damned cent!" he said.

MARRIAGE

Husband: "For twenty years, my wife and I were ecstatically happy."
Friend: "Then what happened?"
Husband: "We met!"

* * * * *

Salesman to a friend: "My wife and I have been happily married for 15 years. As a matter of fact, we go out twice a week, have steak, champagne and dance."
Envious friend: "That's marvelous!"
Salesman: "It certainly is! My wife goes on Mondays and I go on Thursdays."

* * * * *

I know the perfect wedded couple: a manicurist married to a podiatrist. Now they wait on each other hand and foot.

* * * * *

When a woman says to the minister, "I do," she gets half of everything a man owns. When she says to the judge, "I don't," she usually gets the other half.

* * * * *

A 76-year-old man had just taken his seventh wife. A young friend asked him: "Why in the world would an old man like you want to get married for the seventh time?"

"Son," he said, "for the little bit they eat I wouldn't want to be without one."

* * * * *

An old man of 75 married a young girl of 25.

When they came back from the honeymoon two weeks later, the gal looked as if she'd been hit by a truck.

Her girl-friend asked: "What happened to you?"

The bride answered: "When we were courting, he told me that he'd been saving up for 45 years. I thought he meant *money*!"

* * * * *

They were married for twenty-five years and had their biggest argument on the day of their silver anniversary. "If it weren't for my money, that TV set wouldn't be here. If it weren't for my money, the very chair you're sitting on wouldn't be here!"

"Are you kidding?" she interrupted, "if it weren't for your money, I wouldn't be here!"

* * * * *

Fellow ran into the fire engine house and very excitedly shouted: "I'm sorry to bother you, but my wife has disappeared again."

"That's too bad, but why tell us? Why not notify the police?"

"Well, I'll tell you. I told the police the last time she disappeared and they went and found her."

* * * * *

A hopeful young lady visited a computer dating service and listed her requirements: She wanted someone who liked people, was small, preferred formal attire and enjoyed water sports. The computer followed her wishes to the letter. It sent her a penguin.

*   *   *   *   *

Talk about being generous. Why, I knew a guy who was so generous with his girl friend that he finally had to marry her for his money.

*   *   *   *   *

Some people are funny! I knew of a man who hadn't kissed his wife for 10 years, but he went and shot the fellow who did.

*   *   *   *   *

"This is your fourth marriage," said an acquaintance to the divorcee, "first to a banker, then to an actor, then to a minister, and now to an undertaker. Why did you marry men in these particular jobs?"

"Oh, that's easy. One for the money, two for the show, three to get ready, and four to go."

*   *   *   *   *

For 30 years, a guy secretly met a gal each Wednesday without his wife ever finding out. His wife passed away and he married his Wednesday gal. Now he doesn't know what to do on Wednesdays.

MEANNESS

I know a guy who can brighten up a whole room just by walking out of it.

*   *   *   *   *

I know a guy who is so mean that every time he throws a beer party he locks the bathroom.

*   *   *   *   *

Later, he'll vote the town dry—and then move.

MEMORY

Patient to psychiatrist: "My memory has failed me completely. I just can't remember things."

Psychiatrist: "When did you begin to notice this?"
Patient: "Notice what?"

MISUNDERSTANDING

The banker's houseboat was sinking off the Florida coast. He radioed for help. Coast Guard picked up his SOS and radioed back: "We are on the way . . . what is your position? . . . we repeat . . . what is your position?" "I'm Executive Vice-President of First National Bank, and please hurry."

* * * * *

During a recent expedition into the wildest part of darkest Africa, a group of explorers came upon a village of primitive savages. In an attempt to make friends, the leader of the explorers tried to tell the natives what it was like in the civilized, outside world.

"Out there," he said, "we love our fellow man."

To this, the natives gave a ringing cry of "Huzzanga!"

Encouraged by this, the explorer continued: "We treat others as we would want them to treat us!"

"Huzzanga!" exclaimed the natives, with much enthusiasm.

"We are peaceful!" said the explorer.

"Huzzanga!" cried the natives.

With a tear running down his cheek, the explorer ended his fine speech: "We come to you as friends, as brothers. So trust us. Open your arms to us, your houses, your hearts. What do you say?"

The air shook with one long, mighty "Huzzanga!"

Greatly pleased by the reception, the leader of the explorers then began talking with the natives' chief.

"I see that you have cattle here," he said. "They are a species with which I'm unfamiliar. May I inspect them?"

"Certainly, come this way," said the chief. "But be careful not to step in the huzzanga."

* * * * *

While visiting our country, a lovely French maiden found herself out of money just as her visa expired.

Unable to pay her passage back to France, she was in despair until an enterprising sailor made her a sporting proposition. "My ship is sailing tonight," he said. "I'll smuggle you aboard, hide you down in the hold and provide you with a mattress, blankets and food. All it will cost you is a little love."

The girl consented and late that night the sailor snuck her on board his vessel. Twice each day, thereafter, the sailor smuggled a large tray of food below decks, took his pleasure with the little French stowaway and departed. The days turned into weeks and the weeks might have turned into months, if the captain hadn't noticed the sailor carrying food below one evening and followed him. After witnessing this unique bit of barter, he waited until the sailor had departed and then confronted the girl, demanding an explanation. She told him the whole story. "Hmmm," mused the captain. "A clever arrangement, and I must say I admire that young seaman's ingenuity. However, Miss, I feel it is only fair to tell you that this is the Staten Island Ferry."

*   *   *   *   *

You have to *listen* to what people are saying.

The other day a fellow asked me if I was in the service.

I said: "Sure! I was a bomber pilot, and I knocked out three ammunitions dumps, four bridges, and a railroad—and then they sent me overseas."

The guy answered: "That's a mighty fine record!"

*   *   *   *   *

"I nearly ran over a pedestrian a few minutes ago—and, I think he was from Miami."

"How did you know that?"

"Well, when he reached the sidewalk, I heard him say something about the sun and the beach."

*   *   *   *   *

The personnel director of an airplane factory received a questionnaire which asked: "How many employees do you have broken down by sex?"

The director wrote back: "Liquor is more of a problem with us."

*   *   *   *   *

Sometimes we're misunderstood.

Little Jimmy, five years old, was watching his minister put some names over the altar in preparation for Sunday morning.

Jimmy was curious and asked: "Reverend Jones, who are the people whose names you are putting over the altar?"

The good Reverend answered: "Jimmy, those are our brothers who died in the service."

Jimmy thought for a minute, and then said: "Which service, Reverend, the nine-thirty, or the eleven o'clock?"

* * * * *

I made a long distance call and when I was through the operator said, "That will be $14.55." I said, "$14.55? I told you to reverse the charges." "All right! That'll be $55.41."

* * * * *

A sweet young thing was trying to telephone her girl-friend at a large company.

She said to the switchboard operator: "I'm trying to locate Mary Sexauer. Do you have a Sexauer there?"

"Honey," the voice came back, "around here, they don't even give us a coffee break!"

MONEY

Money can't buy everything. It can't buy poverty.

OLD AGE

A very deaf old gentleman decided that a hearing aid was much too expensive, so he got an ordinary piece of wire and wrapped it around his ear.

"Do you hear better now with that wire around your ear?" asked a friend.

"No, but everybody talks louder."

* * * * *

I know a senior citizen who picked up a pacemaker at a dis-

The thing is giving him trouble, though. Every time he his wife, the garage door opens.

* * * * *

Just about the time you learn how to play the game, you're too old to join the team!

* * * * *

I have a neighbor who's 80 years old. His favorite comedy team is Masters and Johnson.

* * * * *

A couple of elderly gents discussing longevity trade secrets—one being 85, the other exactly 100.

Young Feller: "How did *you* live to be a hundred?"

Replied the Elder, "Well, first you get to be 99, then you be careful as hell for a year."

* * * * *

An old mountain man was watching a storekeeper unwrap brightly colored men's pajamas.

"What's that?" he said.

"Pajamas."

"What are they for?"

"You wear them at night. Would you like to buy a pair?"

"Nope! Don't go no place at night except to bed."

* * * * *

Old Mr. Got Rocks, fairly spry for his age, felt it necessary to resist the advances of an impoverished but eager widow of 32. "Mother and Father are against it," he said gravely to her.

"You are not going to tell me your mother and father are still alive?"

"I am referring to Mother Nature and Father Time."

* * * * *

The secret of staying young is to live honestly, eat slowly, sleep sufficiently, work industriously, worship faithfully, and then lie about your age.

OVERSELLING

It's possible to *over*sell your prospect.

A young Catholic girl was in love with a Methodist boy, but thought problems might develop if they got married because of the difference in their religions.

Her mother suggested: "Why don't you convert him to Catholicism? Then there won't be any differences. And now's the time to do it. He'll never be in a better mood to buy!"

Her daughter agreed and reported to her mother a short time later that she'd succeeded; he was converted and all was well.

But just after that the girl came home one day and burst into the house sobbing: "It's all over between us! We're all through!"

The mother said: "I thought you had him sold!"

The girl cried: "I guess I *over*sold him, Mom. Now he's going to be a priest!"

POPULARITY

A young kid had his first crack at the big leagues. Boy, did he want to play! But the coach wasn't taking any chances with an unproven rookie.

Finally, in the ninth inning, with the score tied and three men on base, the youngster pleaded: "Please, Coach, let me go in there and win this game!"

The Manager said: "If you strike out they'll boo you, they'll throw coke bottles, they'll chase you out of the park! But . . . okay, I'll give you a chance."

So the kid went in—and promptly struck out.

The Manager picked him up by the collar and said: "See! I told you! They're booing, they're throwing coke bottles, they *hate* you!"

The kid looked up and smiled. "You got it wrong, Coach. They're not booing *me*. They love me! They're booing *you* for sending me in!"

POSITIVE ATTITUDE

As a sales manager, I once made a call with my local representative in Buffalo, New York.

As we were about to enter the Purchasing Agent's office, the salesman turned to me and said: "This is a very tough buyer, and I don't think I can sell him."

I was aghast at this, and said: "After all I've taught you about having a positive attitude, you stand there and tell me you don't think you can sell him! That's a negative attitude! For heaven's sake, man, be *positive!*"

He immediately retorted: "I guess you're right; I'm *positive* I can't sell him!"

PRICE

Price just isn't that important—except to some people.

A guy in Hollywood was offered a baby elephant for $500.

"An elephant!" he cried. "What in the world would I want with an elephant?"

"Yes, but it's only $500."

"I know! But I don't *want* an elephant!"

"Okay, I'll let you have two for $850."

"It's a deal!"

RELIGION

A sign on a board outside the church said: "If you're tired of sin, come on in."

Some enterprising somebody, with what appeared to be a stick of lipstick, wrote underneath: "If not, call XXX-XXXX."

* * * * *

I knew a man who was in church only three times—when he was baptized, when he was married and when he was buried . . . Hatched, matched, and dispatched.

* * * * *

The ecumenical movement is really taking hold. I heard about it just the other day from Bishop Ginsberg.

*   *   *   *   *

One Sunday morning in Passaic, New Jersey, a Catholic Priest was looking out the parish window and saw a fantastic sight. He just couldn't believe his eyes. So he got on a hot-line to the Vatican and a tired voice answered—there was a change in time, of course.

The Priest said: "Your Holiness, I hate to bother you, but you just have to hear me out. I'm calling from the Blessed Sacrament Church in Passaic, New Jersey, and this tremendous crowd is coming toward me—getting bigger all the time.

"And leading the group is this magnificent figure of a man. He has love and compassion in his eyes. He's wearing a white robe. He's carrying a shepherd's crook. He's wearing sandals. He has a long beard. He passes his hands across the blind and they see. He touches the lame and the crippled and they walk again. Good Heavens, Your Holiness, *what should I do?*"

And the voice at the other end answered: "Look busy. It might be the Boss!"

*   *   *   *   *

A salesman pulled into a motel after a hard day and as he was registering, he casually asked the manager, "Do you have TV in your rooms?" "No," replied the manager. "We belong to a particular religious group and we don't believe in TV." "That's O.K., it's not that important," said the salesman.

As he was hanging up his clothes, he noted that there were no telephones in the rooms; made mental note of it and then walked over to the restaurant.

"I sometimes like to eat breakfast at night. It tastes better. Bring me some ham and eggs," said the salesman to the waitress.

"I'm sorry," said Lucille, "we belong to a particular religious group and we don't eat anything that comes from animal or fowl."

"Well, I wasn't particularly hungry. Just bring me a cup of coffee," he said.

"Sorry, it has caffeine and our group doesn't believe in coffee," said the waitress.

"Tea?" questioned the salesman. "Nope," said Lucille.

"Forget it," said the salesman. "Where's your cigarette machine?"

"Well, our particular religious group . . . ." said Lucille.

"Hold it. I may see you later," remarked the salesman.

He walked back over to the office and spoke to the manager, "I notice that you don't have any telephones in the room and I am a very heavy sleeper. Could you lend me an alarm clock?" This is a common practice in small motels.

"I am terribly sorry," said the manager, "but, our particular religious group doesn't believe in alarm clocks. . . ."

The salesman said, "Look friend, I know what all you *don't* believe in. Would you mind telling me what you *do* believe in?"

The manager replied, "Not at all. We believe in being sweet and kind to each other and we are really just sitting here waiting for the second coming of Christ."

Leaning forward on the counter, the salesman advised, "Let me tell you one thing, Buddy. If *HE* has ever been *here* before. . . .*HE AIN'T COMING BACK!*"

RESPONSIBILITIES

We all make our own decisions as to what we want in life.

The other day, a fellow tried to sell me a 350-pound gorilla.

"What in the world would I want with a gorilla?" I asked him.

"I know what you mean," he said, "but I can let you have this gorilla for only $200."

"O.K.," I said. "It's a bargain. But a 350-pound gorilla in my house! Where in the world will he sleep?"

"Anywhere he wants to—anywhere he wants to!"

SALESMEN

A poor salesman was seen in a motel restaurant lunching on some very thin soup.

A friend asked: "Are you on a diet?"

"No," he said, "on a commission."

*   *   *   *   *

There's a big difference between a *planned* presentation and a *canned* sales pitch.

I heard about a young fellow who was selling typewriters. He made a call on a sales manager and did everything *wrong*. He hemmed and hawed, spilled things on the desk, loused up the demonstration . . . everything was wrong.

The prospect—this sales manager—said: "Son, how long have you been selling?"

"Oh, a couple of weeks."

The sales manager said: "Well, I feel sorry for you. And I feel sorry for your boss—I've got clunks like you, too!—your boss ought to give you a *planned presentation*. See, first you should say this, then you should say that, then you ought to demonstrate the machine just like so, and then you should hand me the order form with a pen. And, just to prove that this would work, I'll sign the order. Now, you take this back to your boss and tell him to give you a *planned presentation*."

The kid said "He has—lots of 'em. *This is the one we use on sales managers!*"

* * * * *

If you want to make ends meet, you'd better start out by getting off *yours!*

* * * * *

It's just like working in a lead mine. All you have to do is *get the lead out.*

* * * * *

Some salesmen are colorful—*yellow.*

* * * * *

The vacuum cleaner salesman walked into his prospect's living room, dropped ten pounds of dirt on the carpet, and said: "In just five minutes I can clean this up so it'll look like new!"

The prospect answered: "You could have—if we'd have paid our electric bill!"

* * * * *

The president and sales manager were looking gloomily at a

map of their territory, with pins showing the locations of salesmen.

"Frankly," said the sales manager to the president, "I think we have only one choice. Let's take the pins out of the map and stick 'em in the salesmen!"

* * * * *

Like the salesman said: "If Russia wants any more territory, they can have mine!"

* * * * *

The salesman had finally agreed to take his wife on his next selling trip. Entering the hotel elevator at the first stop, a sexy-looking blonde, waiting in the elevator, looked at them in surprise and said, "Hi John, how are you?"

When the salesman and his wife reached their room, she demanded, "Who was that broad?"

"Don't make matters worse, Helen," replied the husband, "I'm going to have plenty of trouble explaining you to her!"

* * * * *

Recently, a vice-president in charge of marketing sent the following directive to all salesmen:

"Effective immediately, you are to desist having vodka-based cocktails with customers. If you must drink, order drinks that leave a breath that tells. Therefore, your customer will realize that you are drunk, not stupid."

* * * * *

A man wrote in to a company saying, "I'm interested in your product but don't send any salesman." Two days later, a salesman appeared.

The man said, "I thought I said no salesman!"

"Sir, I'm the closest thing to 'no salesman' that we have."

* * * * *

After a few years of marriage, the young salesman began to spend many evenings out with other salesmen.

One night his conscience bothered him so he called his wife from his office.

"Hello, darling," he said. "Slip on your party clothes and meet me downtown. We'll have dinner at some quiet place and then we'll see a show. How about it?"

"I'd be delighted to meet you, Bob," she replied, "But why not come out to the house and get me? There's nobody home."

Now, hubby spends every night at home. His name is Henry.

* * * * *

The sales manager had been admonishing his salesmen to make more calls. One morning a salesman excitedly reported, "Boss! I made 39 calls yesterday. I would have made more, but some character asked me what I was selling!"

* * * * *

The traveling salesman was asked why he had his wife with him on all his selling trips.

The salesman quickly answered, "I'd rather bring her with me than have to kiss her good-bye!"

* * * * *

The new salesman was on his first sales trip way out in the hinterlands of his not too great territory.

The next morning when he awakened he was shocked to find out that during the night a huge snowstorm had literally snowed him in. Very nervously he telephoned his extra mean sales manager back at the home office.

"Mr. Jones, this is John. I'm snowed in up here in Hinterland. What should I do?"

"Anyone within walking distance you can call on?"

"No sir!"

"Spend the day addressing some advertising pieces to your prospects, then."

"I'm sorry, sir, but I don't have any advertising with me."

"Well," grunted the boss, "you're now taking your first week of vacation."

* * * * *

When a salesman quits during the afternoon and goes to a matinee movie, psychologists tell us that he's going back to the safe, dark comfort of his mother's womb—which, if you want my opinion, is a helluva place to eat popcorn!

* * * * *

"Sorry, sir," said the hotel desk clerk to the traveling salesman, "but we have no rooms at all, unless . . ."

"Unless what?"

"Unless you'd be willing to share a bedroom with a red-headed school teacher."

"Look," said the salesman, "I know you've heard stories about traveling salesmen, but I'll have you know that I'm a happily married church-going, home-loving man!"

"Well," said the clerk, "so is he!"

* * * * *

The new traveling salesman was chatting with an old timer on the road, who asked him how he was doing.

"Not so good," said the new man. "Everyplace I go, I get insulted."

"That's funny," said the old timer. "I've been traveling for more than forty years and I've had my samples pitched out the door, been thrown out myself, kicked down stairs and was even punched in the nose once—but I was never insulted."

* * * * *

Inept salesman: "Will I be getting a raise soon?"

Sales manager: "Of course you will be getting a raise, and it will be effective just as soon as you are."

* * * * *

If he sold a certain suit in stock, the apprentice salesman was told he could have a steady job as a clothing salesman. The suit in question was a beauty—light purple with thin white stripes and yellow dots.

An hour later, clothes in disarray and bloody, he rushed to the manager and shouted, "I sold it!"

"Looks as if you had a lot of customer resistance," said the boss.

"No, I didn't have any trouble with the customer," the young man explained, "but what a fight I had with his seeing-eye dog!"

* * * * *

A salesman called on a prospect with a new item . . . made a beautiful presentation.

"That sounds pretty good, young fellow," said the prospect. "But I want to think it over. Come back and see me next week."

"That's O.K., Sir," said the salesman. "I wish I had a hundred like you!" And he left.

Next week the salesman returned and went through the same presentation. "That sure sounds great," said the prospect. "But I still want to think about it some more. Come back next week."

"That's O.K., Sir. I wish I had a hundred like you!" And he left.

And that went on and on. Finally, the prospect couldn't stand it any longer. He said to this guy: "You've been calling on me for seven months, I've never given you ten cents and you always smile and say: 'I wish I had a hundred like you!' Why?"

The salesman said: "Because, man, I've got a *thousand* like you!"

* * * * *

The inept salesman reported to his sales manager, "I got two orders today—'Get out!' and 'Stay out!' "

SAVOIR-FAIRE

The French have a thing they call "savoir-faire"—it's just hard to explain; even *they're* not sure what it means.

Three Frenchmen were arguing about it. One said: "If you come home and find your wife in another man's arms and you say, 'Excuse me,' that's savoir-faire."

"Oh, no," said the second, more experienced Frenchman. "If you come home and find your wife in another man's arms and you say, 'Excuse me, proceed,' *that's* savoir-faire!"

The third Frenchman, still older and wiser, said, "I don't

think either of you understands. If you come home and find your wife in another man's arms and you say, 'Excuse me, proceed,' *and he proceeds*, then *he* has savoir-faire!"

SELF-AWARENESS

A western rancher had three bulls. A senior bull he had had for many years, another he had for a shorter period of time and one he had only for a brief time. Being anxious to continually improve his herd strain, he was heard by the bulls to say one day he was going to buy another bull. Taking note of this, the senior one said: "54 of the cows on this ranch are *mine* and I want you to know that I'll not share them with *any other* animal!"

The second one said: "Well, 21 of the cows on this ranch are *mine*, and I'm not about to share *them*, either!"

The third one said: "I've been here only a short time and only 5 of the cows are mine, and I'm not about to give any of *them* up!"

When the rancher unloaded his newly acquired animal, he was something to behold! A *giant* of a bull with long tapering horns that gleamed in the summer sun—and he didn't look *through* the fence at the other bulls, he looked *over* at them. At which point, the senior one said: "On second thought, I just may want to share some of my cows with this new friend of ours. He looks deserving." And the second one replied: "Well, if you are going to be so generous, I'll share some of mine, too. I'll give up about 11 of my cows." At this point, the junior bull began to paw the ground and bellow and wring his tail and snort, while the other two, (watching his antics) said: "What in the world are you doing?" He retorted, "I just want to make darn sure he *knows* I'm a *bull*.

SHOW BUSINESS

The helplessly overworked, dirty, uncomfortable, poor slob was finishing up another full day of cleaning out the manure from the elephant pens at the circus ground. A friend was watching him and finally asked: "Why in the world would you keep working on a miserable job like that? Why don't you quit this? There are plenty of other things you could do."

"What!" the poor slob exclaimed in shock, "and quit show business?"

SHYNESS

I know a guy so shy he couldn't lead a group in silent prayer.

* * * * *

He never played football, because everytime he saw the guys in a huddle he thought they were making fun of him.

SPECIALIZATION

This is the age of specialization.

Two guys were arguing about this, and one said: "I'll bet at the National Biscuit Company they even have a Vice President in charge of Fig Newtons!"

The other guy said: "You got to be kidding! I don't believe it." The first fella insisted.

So they bet $20 on it, and to settle the bet called the National Biscuit Company long distance. "We want to talk to the Vice President of Fig Newtons," they said.

The voice came back: "Packaged or loose?"

* * * * *

Another fella asked a chicken farmer: "How do you tell the difference between the little boy chicks and the little girl chicks?"

The farmer said: "That's easy. You put a plate of worms in front of them. Invariably, the little girl chicks will eat the little boy worms, and the little boy chicks will eat the little girl worms!"

"Yes, but how do you tell the difference between the little boy worms and the little girl worms?"

"Hell, man," said the farmer, "I'm a chicken specialist, not a worm specialist."

STRIKES

Even the grave diggers are on strike. I saw them carrying a sign that said: "Nobody gets lowered till we get raised."

SUCCESS

The road to success is always under construction.

* * * * *

Winners like to associate with winners.

I had dinner the other evening with one of the sharpest, most aggressive insurance agents in America. He happened to be from Boston, Massachusetts.

When the time came to order, being a transplanted Texan, I ordered the finest steak on the menu. Not my New England friend; he selected, predictably, fresh lobster.

When the main course was served, my steak was perfect, but my friend's lobster happened to have one claw missing. Would this aggressive insurance man challenge his serving? You'd better believe it!

He grabbed the waiter, pointed to the deformed lobster and demanded: "What's with this *one claw* business?"

The waiter, obviously a quality salesman himself, was equal to the occasion.

"What's a little claw?" he asked, "when considering the fact that this is perhaps the freshest lobster being served anywhere in America tonight. Consider that at the crack of dawn this morning, this delightful lobster was securely nested in a lobster pot off the coast of Maine . . . and the fact that before the sun was high in the sky, this very lobster had been collected and was flown here by jetliner, with loving care by the airline . . . so that you, Sir, could have the succulent freshness of a one-of-a-kind lobster. Granted that during the flight, some of the lobsters become a trifle irritated on occasion, and they tend to joust about and engage in a degree of combat . . . *but* . . . yours is the finest, freshest . . ."

Before the waiter could continue, the agent raised his hand and interjected:

"So he's North Atlantic fresh . . . wonderful! So he's airborne to the city when most others come overland by truck . . . well and good. And if he wants to get into a fight with his friend en route . . . I have no reason to complain. But I do have one request, my man; take this one back to the kitchen, and *bring me the winner!*"

TODAY'S WORLD

Everything we earn, they subtract a tax.
Everything we buy, they add a tax on.

* * * * *

The greatest things in life are the *simple* things.
If you tried to invent a clothes pin today, it wouldn't sell unless it had six transistors, twenty-seven moving parts, and had to be serviced twice a year!

* * * * *

Too many parents send their kids to camp—and their dogs to obedience school.

* * * * *

Things are different today. Times change.
I can remember when the air was clean, sex was dirty—and hot pants was a condition.

* * * * *

There are too many kids who don't believe in Santa Claus—and too many adults who do.

* * * * *

Actually, this is a metallic age—silver in our hair, gold in our teeth, and lead in our pants.

* * * * *

We're living in great times. Never before in history have so many, lived so well, so far behind.

* * * * *

Freight car loading is down eight percent and liquor

consumption is up nine percent—which only means that more people are getting loaded than freight cars.

*   *   *   *   *

Of course, more people are living together these days without getting married. So the jewelry manufacturers are selling Shacking-Up Rings as well as Wedding Rings. The names of the couple are engraved on special inserts—removable so they can be changed along with the changes in personnel.

TROUBLES

Never tell people about your troubles. 80% don't care—and the other 20% are *glad* you're more miserable than they are.

WIVES

"I just got a Cadillac for my wife."
"Wish I could get a deal like that!"

*   *   *   *   *

"My wife has a very bad memory."
"Forgets everything?"
"No, she remembers everything!"

*   *   *   *   *

Doctor: "You won't last a week if you don't stop running around with women."
Patient: "Oh, there is nothing wrong with me. I'm in great shape."
Doctor: "Yeah, I know, but one of those women is my wife."

*   *   *   *   *

Arriving home unexpectedly, Henry found his wife in the arms of his best friend. "Well, I'm glad to finally have this out," exclaimed the friend. "I love your wife and want her for my own. Let's be gentlemen and settle this with a game of cards. Winner takes Emily, all right? Shall we play gin rummy?"

"Sounds fine to me, but how about a penny a point just to make the game interesting?"

* * * * *

My wife is a stickler for neatness. I get up in the middle of the night to go to the bathroom. When I come back, the bed's made.

* * * * *

My wife had plastic surgery. I cut up all her credit cards.

* * * * *

A guy wrote a letter to another guy: "I understand you've been fooling around with my wife—and *I don't like it.* Meet me here in my office next Monday at 10:00 a.m. and we'll settle this like gentlemen."

The other guy wrote back: "I received your form letter. Unfortunately I'll be unable to attend the meeting—but whatever the rest decide is okay with me!"

* * * * *

My wife bugged me so long for a mink, I finally got her one. Now she won't even clean out the cage.

* * * * *

A guy comes home one night, finds his wife in the sack with another man.

He's enraged! "What in the world are you *doing?*" he roars. The wife turns to her lover. "See, I told you he was stupid!"

* * * * *

A fellow and his wife were about to go to a masquerade party at the country club; she was going as Cinderella, and he was dressed as the handsome prince.

But just as they were about to leave the house, she got a terrible headache, and decided to stay home and go to bed. But, not wanting to spoil her good husband's evening, she urged him to attend without her—which he did.

The scene changes.

Two hours later and a couple of aspirins later, the wife felt better and decided to join the party.

The club was alive with festivity. And in the center of the crowd, this good lady, in her Cinderella costume, saw her handsome prince. She sidled up to him.

"Would you like to dance?" she asked.

"Don't mind if I do," he said. And they danced up a storm.

When the music ended, she asked: "Would you like to take a walk in the moonlight?"

"Don't mind if I do," he said. And they walked, hand in hand, in the moonlight.

The next part of the story is censored.

Three hours later, as they climbed into bed at home, the wife asked coyly: "Did you enjoy the party, dear?"

"Hell, no!" the husband answered. "I got into a poker game in the locker room, and Charlie Jones won all my money—including that damned prince costume!"

WOMEN

I met this girl in 1972. Not the year—the hotel room.

* * * * *

She said she liked to live life up to the hilt. So that's where I took her—the Conrad Hilt.

* * * * *

The secretary rushed into the executive's office. "I've got some good news and some bad news," she shouted.

"I'm up to here with bad news," he said. "What's the good news?"

"Well, at least you're not sterile!"

*   *   *   *   *

The father of a lovely 18-year-old girl found out that his daughter had hitchhiked alone from Seattle to San Diego.

"You could have been molested, assaulted, or raped," he said.

"I was perfectly safe," she said, "Every time a lone man picked me up I always told him I was going to San Diego because it had the best VD clinic on the West Coast."

*   *   *   *   *

"Do you mind if I try that dress on in the window?" asked the customer.

"Not at all, madame," replied the clerk, "but wouldn't you rather use the dressing room?"

*   *   *   *   *

Never call a woman an old maid. They are unclaimed jewels. One I know said: "When I die, I don't want any men for my pall-bearers. If they can't take me out when I'm alive, they're not gonna take me out after I'm gone."

*   *   *   *   *

Conversation over hotel phone:
"Is this Tom Jones?"
"Yes."
"Tom Jones with the Boilermakers Convention?"
"That's right."
"Were you playing around with Suzy Smith last night?"
"Well, as a matter of fact, I was."
"Well, this is *Mr*. Smith, and I don't like it!"
"Tell you the truth, I didn't think much of it myself!"

*   *   *   *   *

Three young women were attending the same logic class given at one of the better universities. During a lecture, the professor stated that he was going to test their ability at situation reasoning.

"Let us assume," said the professor, "that you are aboard a small craft alone in the Pacific, and you spot a vessel approaching you with several thousand sex-starved sailors on board. What would you do in this situation to avoid any problem?"

"I would attempt to turn my craft in the opposite direction," stated the redhead.

"I would pass them, trusting my knife to keep me safe," responded the brunette.

"Frankly," murmured the blonde, "I understand the situation, but I fail to see the problem."

WORK

My boss only wants me to work a half-day—and he doesn't care which 12 hours that is.

Index
Ready-Reference
Story-Tellers Guide

Index

205